JESUS *and* DIVORCE

*A Biblical Guide
for Ministry
to Divorced Persons*

GEORGE R. EWALD
Foreword by Willard M. Swartley

HERALD PRESS
Waterloo, Ontario
Scottdale, Pennsylvania

Canadian Cataloguing-in-Publication Data
Ewald, George R., 1931-
  Jesus and divorce

Includes bibliographical references and index.
ISBN 0-8361-3572-5

1. Jesus Christ—Views on divorce. 2. Divorce—Biblical teaching.
3. Divorce—Religious aspects—Christianity. 4. Church work with
divorced people. I. Title.

BS2417.D6E8 1991   241'.63   C91-095190-X

JESUS AND DIVORCE
Copyright © 1991 by Herald Press, Waterloo, Ont. N2L 6H7
  Published simultaneously in the United States by Herald Press,
  Scottdale, Pa. 15683. All rights reserved.
Library of Congress Catalog Number: 91-75419
International Standard Book Number: 0-8361-3572-5
Printed in the United States of America
Book and cover design by Gwen M. Stamm
Cover photo by Jean-Claude Lejeune

99 98 97 96 95 94 93 92 91 10 9 8 7 6 5 4 3 2 1

To my wife, Shirl,
my best friend and devoted partner in life,
and to those caring pastors
who work to ease the burdens
of hurting people

Contents

Foreword

As the churches over the last half century have become more assimilated into the dominant culture of the West, the pressures of modern life have taken a toll upon their marriages and family life. Amidst this process, congregations have increasingly heeded the call to mission and opened their doors to people seeking church membership who were already divorced and remarried.

This volume comes as the fourth Herald Press book addressing the difficult topic of divorce and remarriage. It thus extends the contribution of J. C. Wenger's *Dealing Redemptively with Those Involved in Divorce and Remarriage Problems* (1965), John R. Martin's *Divorce and Remarriage* (1974), and Edwin Bontrager's *Divorce and the Faithful Church* (1978). Ewald now contributes additional dimensions for us to consider. This book contains aspects of biblical study that will be relatively new for many readers.

Of the many commendable features of this study, I highlight four that merit special notice. First, Ewald's study of Jewish practices regarding divorce and remarriage is especially helpful in understanding Jesus' teaching and its significance.

Second, Ewald rightly locates our understanding of Jesus' teachings against divorce within the broader profile of Jesus' mission and message. Jesus consistently critiqued Pharasaic legalism and compassionately associated, even at table fellowship, with sinners and marginalized people. As Ewald contends, our understanding of Jesus' teachings on divorce and remarriage must be brought into line with this larger central portrait of who Jesus was and what he stood for.

Third, Ewald offers numerous helpful suggestions at the practical level for both persons and congregations facing divorce and remarriage. While never slighting the reality of sin in divorce's failure to achieve God's will for marriage, Ewald provides an outline for a service whereby a congregation can participate redemptively in the midst of the divorce tragedy. At another place he provocatively proposes that "remarriage can become a redemptive occasion."

Fourth, toward the end of the book, Ewald leads the readers to consider ways to strengthen marriage and prevent divorce. Especially noteworthy are his discussions of Pastoral and Congregational Care for the Divorced (in chapter 13) and Preventative Programs for the Church (in chapter 14).

The book also includes a Leader's Guide, which makes it useful as a study for a Sunday school quarter. Too often our congregations handle the issue of divorce and remarriage like the priest and Levite treated the wounded man by the roadside. We "pass by," either by not getting involved, or we simply accept the increasing number of divorces and remarriages as commonplace. Both reactions fall short of the good Samaritan response of compassion, care, and health (Luke 10:29-37).

In addition to the many excellent insights Ewald brings to us in this book, I encourage consideration of two additional issues as part of the study process. First, I believe we must sensitize Christians in marriage to the strategies of Satan to "get at" the marriage and ruin it. (The number one goal adopted at a national Satanist convention in 1988 was to destroy Christian marriages, especially those of Christian leaders.) Second, I suggest that the study process include some critique of the individualism of our Western world and its impact upon marriage successes and failures. In the June 1991 *Theology News and Notes* of Fuller Theological Seminary, a Kenyan church leader says that in his forty years he has not seen one African Christian who has been divorced. In his culture the community takes responsibility for the marriage. The best man and woman at the wedding supply ongoing nurture and counsel to the married couple and enlist the larger community to resolve problems that arise.

I heartily recommend Ewald's fine contribution. I agree with all major points in his biblical interpretation—the excepting clause, divorce and remarriage in Jewish culture, our understandings of Paul's teachings, and Jesus as model. I am happy to commend this book to the church for prayerful study and the compassionate care for one another to which this contribution calls us.

—*Willard M. Swartley*
Professor of New Testament
Associated Mennonite Biblical Seminaries
Elkhart, Indiana
July 1991

Preface

The denomination with which I ministered for twenty-seven years has struggled with the question of whether its pastors could perform marriages for divorced people. Delegates face this question at almost every biennial conference, and still their policy forbids such participation. About fifteen years ago, the denomination's sister organization in the United States had arrived at a policy permitting ministers to perform marriages for the party not guilty of adultery, but not for other divorced persons. This position was not comfortable to myself nor to the denomination I served at that time.

As I taught counseling and pastoral theology in Bible college, I was forced into deeper study of the subject. Eventually, on sabbatical I began work on a thesis in a Master of Sacred Theology program at Lutheran Theological Seminary, Saskatoon, Saskatchewan, Canada. This book is a revision of that 305-page thesis. I would like to acknowledge the helpful contribution of my two thesis advisers at the seminary, Dr. Erwin Buck and Dr. Walter Koehler, and also Mrs. Eleanor Morrison of Peterborough, Ontario, who did such an able job of typing the thesis. My sincere appreciation and gratitude goes out to them.

I also want to thank Shirl, my wife of thirty-six years, who has stood by my side through six pastorates and eleven years of Bible college teaching. Her love and encouragement have meant so much to me, as together we have endeavored to serve the Lord in ministry.

Over the years my heart has gone out to those pastors who have felt compassion in their hearts toward those divorced. These church leaders wanted to help them rebuild their lives and to assist them into the life and love of the church. Yet, the pastors struggled with church policies, their own interpretations of the words of Jesus, and even guilt. Therefore, they failed to really be able to extend the grace of God in their hearts to those hurting from divorce.

Such ministers would send divorced persons down the street to another pastor who could marry them, or they would send them to a justice of the peace. They could accept the divorced into membership, but they couldn't use them in certain leadership positions in the church. As a result, divorced persons felt like second-class citizens in the congregation. As a teacher who had to help aspiring ministers to cope with these dilemmas, I determined to discover the impact that the abuse of the patriarchal right by the husband had upon the interpretation of Jesus' words. *Jesus and Divorce* is the result of that study. I trust that it will liberate many to freedom of ministry in faithfulness to the Word.

A Field Trip into Bible Times

Churches, pastors, and denominations have all struggled with the divorce dilemma. They desire to minister, to help, to forgive, and to accept. But this has been countered and held in tension by the traditional understanding that Jesus' words on divorce were legalisms that forbade divorce and required celibacy following it.

This book looks for an answer to that tension. In doing so, we will take a journey back into pre-Mosaic times to observe marriage customs in the time of the patriarchs, and then move on to the era of Moses. We will examine laws which show divine concern for the sanctity of marriage, and we will also see laws which give evidence of the mercy of God and God's concern for wives who were abused by insensitive and selfish husbands.

Next we will view the traditions of the Jewish Talmud regarding marriage and divorce, as these teachings developed into the time of the Pharisees of Jesus' day and beyond. The scenery will include drama of interaction, tension, and conflict between Jesus and the Pharisees. This will reveal the character and feelings of two schools of Pharisees, one under the rigid and temporarily more dominant Shammai, and the other under the more liberal and humane Hillel. In the light of this background, we will be prepared to interpret the testing of Jesus by the Pharisees on the question of divorce and his answers to them.

We will observe the Friend of sinners, the one who ate with publicans and outcasts and accepted the devotion of a prostitute. Again we will be impressed that Jesus is the one who fulfilled God's law and also modeled God's grace. This experience will bring us to a conclusion in our own mind and heart that will free us for ministry to the hurting, depressed, and disappointed of our day. Alongside the Master, we will be prepared to minister to those who have known the agony and hurt, the shame and grief, and the awful frustration of divorce.

Once we have made this discovery, we will be ready to benefit from the practical guidelines for the church near the end of this book.

—*George R. Ewald*
Chatham, Ontario
Canada

1

Jewish Marriage Customs and Patriarchy

Our goal is fully to appreciate the living situation into which Jesus spoke on adultery, marriage, and divorce. We therefore need to understand Jewish law and practice on these matters.

Jewish Law on Marriage

Polygamy (polygyny, having more than one wife) and divorce were both accepted customs in ancient Near Eastern society prior to the founding of the Jewish nation or the writing of the Hebrew Scriptures.[1] The Old Testament laws do not establish polygamy or divorce. Instead, they regulate those practices to protect the individual who may be abused by unkind treatment.

In the Old Testament, kings often have large harems. Monogamy is the prevailing form of marriage for other people. Yet it is taken for granted that a man may have two wives, or a wife and a concubine, especially if the first partner does not conceive enough children. On one hand, that helps to fulfill the command to multiply and fill the earth (Gen. 1:28). But on the other hand, it demonstrates the power of the male over the female and provides many occasions for marital unhappiness and abuse of the wife caught in the system.

Polygamy is frequently the indirect cause of turmoil, stress, and the breakdown of God's highest intentions for marriage as expressed in Genesis 2:24, where a husband "clings to his wife, and they become one flesh." A man may have a hated wife and a loved wife. The case law of Deuteronomy 21:15-17 protects the rights of the son of the hated wife, if he is the firstborn, by ensuring that he receives a double portion of the inheritance.

Lamech, the son of Methushael, is the first mentioned in the Bible with multiple wives (Gen. 4:19). Abraham takes his wife's maid, Hagar, as a concubine (Gen. 16:1-2). Esau and Jacob each have more than one wife (Gen. 28:9; 29:15-30). Gideon has many wives and seventy sons (Judg. 8:30). Elkanah married Hannah and Peninnah (1 Sam. 1). Saul has wives and concubines, as does David (2 Sam. 3:3-5). Solomon is infamous for his seven hundred wives and three hundred concubines (1 Kings 11:3). Ashur, Rehoboam, Abijam, and Jehoiada are all kings with multiple wives.

According to Abraham Cohen,[2] "the Talmud, like the Bible, sanctioned polygamy but discountenanced it. Various opinions on the subject may be culled from its pages: 'A man may marry as many wives as he pleases' (Jeb. 65a), said one authority. 'He may not exceed four' (ibid., 44a), declared another [the view adopted by Muhammad: Koran 14.3]. While yet another rabbi maintained: 'A man must give his wife a divorce if she desires it on his taking an additional wife' (ibid., 65a)." One must study the date of each rabbi to appreciate the period and location for that opinion.

Few Scriptures in the Old Testament take direct issue with polygamy. There is a warning in Deuteronomy 17:17 advising the king not to "acquire many wives for himself, or else his heart will turn away." The message here is not so much against having more than one wife as against rulers taking foreign wives to seal alliances and thereby being attracted to worship other gods (1 Kings 11). Even the New Testament references calling for a bishop or a deacon to be the husband of one wife are likely not prohibitions of polygamy (1 Tim. 3:2, 12; Tit. 1:6). Such was rare among common persons in that day and had been so for some time. More likely those texts expect church leaders to be prime examples of faithfulness within marriage (see on The Pastoral Epistles, in chapter 9).

God is both patient and flexible in dealing with those who have several wives, even though it does not reflect his highest intention. This observation may help us not to interpret New Testament passages more rigidly or legalistically than the way God deals with polygamists of the Old Testament. Under both testaments, God's will and grace needs to be applied to real situations of life.

Obviously, God loves and uses as leaders such great men as Abraham, Jacob, Gideon, David, and Solomon despite their failing to have ideal or exemplary marriages. God certainly does not apply his highest standards for leadership in some legalistic way that leaves no room for exceptions through his grace. Let us keep this in mind!

Marriage is extolled in the writings of Judaism (Song of Sol.). God forms the first couple (Gen. 1:27; 2:24), and that relationship is meant to be characterized by fidelity (Prov. 5:18-23). The Decalogue says, "You shall not commit adultery" (Exod. 20:14). Monogamy is the most common arrangement, though polygamy is in evidence in earlier Judaism if one could afford it. However, by the Christian era, monogamy is virtually the only form of marriage in Judaism. Sources which indicate that monogamy is the accepted form of marriage are the Mishnah and the Zadokite Document from the Dead Sea Scrolls.[3] By the time of Christ, most people's financial circumstances ruled out polygamy.

Celibacy was frowned on by the rabbis, who taught that "a man should marry by eighteen, and if he passed the age of twenty without taking a wife he transgressed a divine command [to multiply and fill the earth; Gen. 1:28] and incurred God's displeasure."[4] They considered having children to be the object of marriage.

A woman's place is in the home of her father until marriage. She has the right to maintenance from the estate of her father, even if it leaves nothing for his sons. She also can claim from his estate a dowry (*ketubah*) equal to that of her elder sisters. When she marries, her dowry becomes the temporary property of her husband. If he divorces his wife without just cause, he likely must return the dowry.[5] By the time of Jesus, the requirement of return of dowry functions to cause the husband to think seriously before proceeding with a divorce. In Judaism, motherhood is the highest calling for a woman (see Luke 1:27-28).

Marriages are usually arranged by the parents. One of the father's duties is to give his son a wife and to get a husband for his daughters. A father may make a betrothal agreement for his daughter while she is still under the age of twelve, but this is to be done with care. "According to the Talmud, 'A man is forbidden to give his daughter in marriage while she is a minor, until she is grown up and says I wish to marry so-and-so' (Kid. 41a)." If he gives her in marriage while she is under twelve, she may repudiate that union on reaching the age of twelve and have it annulled without a divorce.[6] If the betrothal contract is broken beyond the age of twelve, it requires a *get*, a bill of divorcement.[7]

The term for betrothals is *kiddushin*, denoting sanctification, which means that the woman was consecrated or set apart exclusively for her husband. "The husband prohibits his wife to the whole world like an object which is dedicated to the Sanctuary."[8] Chastity is demanded of the wife and implied for the husband. In this one can see marks of the patriarchal system, where the girl or woman is viewed as the property of the male and therefore to be protected by law for and by the male. This kind of authority, unfortunately, often leads to heavy-handed abuse on the part of men, as well as to a double standard of morality. The wife has to be kept for the husband, but the husband is not always kept for the wife.

Marriage is designed to be for life, as shown in Genesis 2:24 (KJV): to "leave" and to "cleave" and to "be one flesh" indicate a permanent relationship for life. Polygamy does not fit God's intention in creation, nor does adultery.

Patriarchal Rights Abused

In a patriarchal society fathers and husbands have supreme authority in their family. In the Old Testament, men are expected to protect and provide for the women in their home. At times, men tend to take advantage of their position of power to the disadvantage of the women. If we understand the abuses of patriarchal rights current in that culture, we will be one step closer to understanding the statements of Jesus on divorce.

Following are some of the patriarchal rights reflected in the Old Testament:

1. Sons have greater independence than daughters.

2. Fathers have responsibility for arranging marriages for both sons and daughters.[9] Daughters are considered the property and responsibility of their fathers, and wives the property and responsibility of their husbands. This is not necessarily a bad thing when the fathers and husbands are thoughtful, loving, and faithful. Sadly, this is not always the case. Many abuses of the power and rights of the male take place. On occasion daughters are married off for political or economic advantage (1 Sam. 18:20-21; Exod. 21:7). To protect his visitors, Lot is prepared to give his daughters to the crowd of lustful men outside his door (Gen. 19:8). Men have exceptional power over their women.

3. A husband can force his wife to go through a trial of jealousy if he is suspicious that she was unfaithful to him, thereby jeopardizing his family line (Num. 5:11-31). This trial is intended to bring God's judgment upon her if she is guilty. It also is to remove any guilt from the husband if he has sexual relationships with his wife while she is carrying on a secret affair (5:31). There is no evidence of concern for the wife who may be suspicious of her husband, and no law to settle such jealousy.

4. A man escapes with relatively light punishment if he is caught while raping an unmarried or unbetrothed woman. He pays the father fifty shekels of silver and is to marry her without the privilege of divorce (Deut. 22:28-29). The reason he has no right to divorce her is because he humbled her. Otherwise, divorce is a right he expects (Deut. 24:1-4). According to Exodus 22:16-17, the father can refuse to give her in marriage, in which case the seducer is required to pay money according to the dowry of virgins.

5. If a man is guilty of adultery with a slave woman betrothed to another, an inquiry is to be held (Lev. 19:20-22). He has the privilege of forgiveness through a guilt offering. When he brings

this offering, the priest makes atonement for him, and his sin is forgiven. Nothing is said of what becomes of the woman. Presumably she is passed on to the other man for whom she was "designated."

6. A man's vow before the Lord must stand, but a woman's vow may be overturned by her father or her husband (Num. 30:1-16).

7. The right of the husband to divorce his wife was established in ancient Near Eastern society before the writing of the Deuteronomic Code. That culture sanctioned "male-order divorce." Arab Muslim practice reflects ancient custom allowing the husband to divorce his wife simply with an oral formula before two witnesses. Hosea 2:2 reflects a typical formula: "You are not my wife, and I am not your husband." The Mishnah prescribes a key statement in a divorce: "Lo, thou art free to marry any man."[10] Mosaic law requires a written document, taking time and money and thus deterring rash action. The accepted procedure is for the husband to deliver to her a *get*, a bill of divorce, as in Deuteronomy 24:1-4.

That certificate of divorce officially ends the marriage and protects the genealogy of the family, which is so important in Jewish society.[11] It also frees the wife for remarriage, usually needed for economic survival. This is the accepted meaning of divorce, both in the period from Abraham to Moses and on into and beyond the time of Jesus. The woman in Jewish society may not divorce her husband, although Hellenistic and Roman laws allow her to do so (Mark 10:12; 1 Cor. 7:13). If she suspects him of desertion, she may go to the elders and sue him to divorce her.[12]

8. For centuries prior to the time of Christ, men had developed their patriarchal privilege to include the putting away of their wives for trivial reasons, even for spoiling a dish, according to Hillel.[13]

Conclusions and Questions

In summary, patriarchy gives the husband and father supreme authority in his home. That leadership can be used in a kind and thoughtful way, in caring for and protecting the women and children of the family. It may also be used in exploitative and abusive ways. Both expressions of patriarchy can be seen in ancient Jewish society. Even today, pastors and social workers often observe men who use the ethos of patriarchy as an excuse for being abusive in their own families.[14]

At its worst, the patriarchal system has been seen by some men to justify a "lord of the manor" attitude. They boss their wives with little sensitivity for their feelings. They see the concept of submission as a biblical basis for giving orders, and they frequently allocate their wives to menial or lesser tasks without due regard to the development of their true giftings or fulfillment. Not only has the wife been seen to be secondary in her role, but until recently, women were seriously hampered in their advancement in the workplace by such an impoverished interpretation of patriarchy.

This model of patriarchy subdues the spirit of the wife; it suggests an inability to act or think independently from her husband. Women raised under this corrupted dominant rule are suppressed, not only in their development, but in their ability to think of themselves as having potential to be developed.

If patriarchy is to survive in this age when women are demanding their rights, it is going to have to adopt a gentler, more sensitive role for itself. In reference to 1 Timothy 3:5, Lorne Shepherd suggests that "manage" or "rule" means an example of loving leadership. "There is no suggestion here of the husband acting like a dictator! Instead, he leads by serving. God is calling a man to lay down his life for his family, to serve them, to set the example and to be responsible (Eph. 5:25-33). He is to follow the example of Jesus, who washed His disciples' feet (John 13:3-20)."[15]

At its best, patriarchy should portray the role of the male as providing a relationship of love, understanding, security, and spiritual strength. This model of patriarchy follows the apostle Paul's counsel in Ephesians 5:25: "Husbands love your wives, just as Christ loved the church, and gave himself up for her." The headship of the husband is reflected, not in dominance and heavy-handed leadership, but in a loving relationship of fidelity in which the man leaves his parents to cleave unto his wife (Eph. 5:31).

The apostle Peter (1 Pet. 3:7) exhorts husbands to love their wives, living with them with special understanding, respecting that they usually are not as strong physically. Just because men may be stronger, they are not to use that strength to their advantage, but rather to protect and give security. "This does not mean that the wife is inferior. It means that she bears children, and that her body is constructed in such a way that she is vulnerable in those times. God instructs men to be understanding and supportive for their wives. The passage continues, 'Remember that you and your wife are partners in receiving God's blessings.' "[16]

The fruit of the Spirit must be active in the successful leadership of any family, and this is especially true of a patriarchal system. Healthy marriages will model interdependence, mutuality, cooperation, respect, and flexibility of responsibilities in accord with the immediate circumstances and gifts of each partner. The gifts and potential of each spouse will be encouraged to fruition. The wise husband and wife will recognize latent skills and ambitions in their spouse and encourage their fulfillment. There is to be a mutual respect and submission each to the other (1 Cor. 11:11-12; Eph. 5:21-33).

An interesting question to ponder from the creation account (Gen. 1:26-28) is whether patriarchy was God's original intention. At that point both male and female are made in the image of God and given a mandate to manage the rest of creation. There is nothing in Genesis 1-2 about one human being ruling another. Is it possible that patriarchy may have been God's response to humanity's Fall into sin (Gen. 3:16)? If so, it is also observable that sin has had its effect on the patriarchal system, which makes it all the more necessary to review that sinful impact and to redress the damage that has been done. Not everyone will favor the viewpoint of Christian feminists, but some of the points they make deserve to be considered in an effort to eliminate the abuses and to balance the bad image that the patriarchal system has earned for itself over the centuries.[17]

A correlative question also needs to be considered. What effect should salvation and new birth have upon our relationships to reverse the effects of the Fall into sin? How does this help us to renew the image of God that is in every woman and man? Are we not called into covenantal relationship with each other and with God, which ought to lead us into deep respect for each other? Paul teaches that the basis for entrance into Christ is the same for male and female (Gal. 3:28). He defends the rights of both husbands and wives to have authority over each others' bodies (1 Cor. 7:2-5). Paul is not abandoning the patriarchal pattern, or the difference in the physical function and roles of the spouses, but could it be that he is laying a foundation for "bringing into reality the true and full partnership of male and female"?[18]

With this brief review of Jewish marriage customs and abuses of patriarchal rights, we now move on to examine Jewish teachings on divorce in more detail.

2

Jewish Law on Divorce

The Pre-Mosaic Patriarchal Right to Divorce

The right for the husband to divorce his wife if "he finds something objectionable about her" (Deut. 24:1) was pre-Mosaic. This patriarchal right to divorce derived from the total authority of the husband in his own home from time immemorial. Both the Laws of Eshnunna and the Code of Hammurabi were before Moses' time and make reference to laws regulating the existing divorce practice.[1]

The Jewish scholar, David Amram, in his fine book, *The Jewish Law of Divorce*, points out that "the origins of the [Jewish divorce] law are to be found in the constitution of the patriarchal family, and the fundamental principle of its government was the absolute authority of the oldest male ascendant, who was the lawgiver and the judge, and whose rule over his wives, children and slaves was supreme."[2] Cohen writes that "this accounts for the ruling which is never disputed in the Talmud: 'A woman may be divorced with or without her consent, but a man can only be divorced with his consent' " (Jeb. 14.1).[3]

Amram contends that the law of divorce "cannot be said to exist in the Biblical code at all. . . ."[4] The few references to it in

22

Deuteronomy grew into volumes of law in the Talmud and other rabbinical writings. Amram continues:

> This ancient right of the husband, to divorce his wife at his pleasure, is the central thought in the entire system of Jewish divorce law; and the Rabbis did not, nor could they, set it aside, although . . . they gradually tempered its severity by numerous restrictive measures. . . . It was not until the eleventh century of the common era that . . . the absolute right of the husband to divorce his wife at will was formally abolished, although it had been practically non-existent in Talmudic times [ff. 215 A.D.].[5]

Deuteronomy Misunderstood

There has been a great deal of misunderstanding and misinterpretation of the law which regulates divorce in Deuteronomy 24:1-4. This misunderstanding is reflected in the question of the Pharisees in Matthew 19:7 and also in the translation of the passage in the *King James Version*. Both suggest that Moses issued a law that the husband should give his wife a bill of divorce if she finds no favor in his eyes. Jesus' response was that Moses "allowed" the putting away of the wife because of the hardness of their hearts, "but from the beginning it was not so" (19:8).

Reliable modern versions (such as NIV, RSV, NRSV, NEB, REB) and the Septuagint (the Greek translation of the Old Testament done by the Alexandrian Jews) all agree with the sense of the passage as follows:

1. If the wife finds no favor in his eyes, and he writes her a bill of divorce and sends her out of his house, and

2. If she goes out and becomes another man's wife, and

3. If the second man dislikes her, writes her a bill of divorce, puts it in her hand, and sends her out of his house, or if the latter husband dies,

4. Then her former husband, who sent her away, may not take her again to be his wife. . . .

On this rendering, there are three conditions before the command in verse four, which then is only to regulate divorce and remarriage. It does not originate a law favoring divorce, as the

Pharisees of Jesus' day suggest. Dr. J. H. Hertz, late Chief Rabbi of the British Empire, comments on the passage:

> What we have here is no law instituting or commanding divorce. This institution is taken for granted, as in Lev. xxi, 7, and Num. xxx, 9-10. We are merely given one regulation in regard to it; viz., that a man who has divorced his wife may not remarry her, if her second husband divorced her or died.[6]

The Deuteronomic Code does not question the use of the divorce bill, but rather allows or suffers it. However, the Jews for many centuries, even into the time of Jesus, became accustomed to using the certificate of divorce as if it were indeed a commandment of Moses. It was the abuse of the divorce bill by the husbands that Jesus called into question in his discussion with the Pharisees.

There is no doubt that the followers of Hillel in Jesus' day and Jewish men for many centuries had assumed that Moses' blessing rested upon the giving of the divorce bill if the wife failed to please her husband. In the process of time, because the patriarchal right to divorce had been incorporated into the Deuteronomic Code, Jewish commentators came to accept the practice as though sanctioned by Moses. It therefore became part of the buildup of oral law surrounding the Mosaic Law.

Something Shameful

The *King James Version* of Deuteronomy 24:1 refers to "some uncleanness" in the wife which does not please the husband. Recent translations are "some indecency" (RSV), "something indecent" (NIV), "offensive" (REB), "shameful" (NEB), or "objectionable" (NRSV).

To the strict followers of Shammai in Jesus' day, that meant sexual immorality on the part of the wife. The Hebrew words *ervath dabar* literally meant *the nakedness of the matter*. On this interpretation, the Shammaites sought to limit divorce to adultery.[7] Their legalism (emphasis on conforming to law or a code of deeds and observances) often put them at odds with Jesus in so many ways. One therefore wonders whether Jesus really was intending to side with them in the use of the so-called exception clauses in Matthew 19:9 and 5:32 (see below, chapters 7-8).

To the followers of Hillel, leader of the more-liberal school of Pharisees often in conflict with the Shammaites, *some shameful thing* didn't mean adultery, since that was punishable by death in the Mosaic Law (Deut. 22:22; Lev. 20:10). Rather, it could be anything that displeased the husband. Only a pretext was needed for divorce; even spoiling a dish of food was sufficient justification. Akiba (ca. A.D. 135) allowed divorce if the husband found another woman more beautiful than his wife.[8]

Solomon Zeitlin, writing about the second Jewish Commonwealth (ca. 37 B.C.–A.D. 66), states that a wife had to be above suspicion. She could be divorced and her *ketubah* (dowry) forfeited if she transgressed the customs of Judea: for example, walking in the street with her head uncovered, speaking with men indiscriminately, or even noisy misdemeanor.[9] Philo, the Alexandrian Jew (A.D. 10-60), believed that the wife could be divorced at any time, but that this was based on ancient customary right, rather than on Deuteronomy 24:1-4.[10] Alfred Edersheim said that "uncleanness" included every kind of impropriety, such as immodesty, indiscreet and bold acts, disrespect, a general bad reputation, or fraud before marriage.[11]

Regardless of the meaning in Deuteronomy 24:1, Jesus responded strongly to any suggestion by Shammaite or Hillelite Pharisees that there was a legalistic basis for divorce: "What God has joined together, let no one separate" (Matt. 19:6).

In summary, there was an ancient patriarchal right to divorce which Jewish men had come to accept as part of the law of Moses. The rule was that if a man was going to divorce his wife, he must give her a certificate of divorce. This bill legally set the woman free from her husband in order that she might remarry. Remarriage was not questioned among the Hebrews (except for the case handled in Deut. 24:4).

The purpose of the document was to ensure that, when a remarriage did occur, the first husband could not change his mind, deny the divorce, and take back his wife, thus rendering her second marriage adulterous. Under the proper use of the divorce bill, the second marriage was not deemed adulterous since the first husband had given up all claims or rights to his first wife. It was only considered adulterous under the conditions of Deuteronomy 24:1-4, in which case it was "abhorrent to the Lord." Marriage was to be inviolable; a man's wife should not be violated. But marriage was not considered indissoluble; the husband claimed the right to dissolve the marriage.

The Positive Side of Divorce

The redemptive side of divorce shows God's concern for the woman. In a strongly patriarchal society, she was at a distinct disadvantage if her husband did not fulfill God's expressed intention for marriage as long as both live (Gen. 1:24; Matt. 19:4-6). Male and female were created in such a way that they can help to fulfill each other within the marriage bond. Patriarchy gave the husband a position of leadership and strength in which he was to love, protect, and provide for his wife. He was to see that both of them would have their social, psychological, physical, and spiritual needs met within their own relationship in union and fellowship with God.

When husbands were selfish and sinful in respect to their marital commitment, then God, through his servant Moses, provided rules to help to alleviate the plight of the disadvantaged wives. There are two key passages that are important in helping the church approach this subject with more tolerance and flexibility. Both are laws which basically command the husband to put away his wife when it is to her advantage. They are concerned with the slave wife and the captive wife.

In Exodus 21:7-11 a number of conditions are set forth restricting abuse against a daughter who is sold into slavery as a secondary wife designate for either the master or his son. If either marries the bondwoman and also has or takes another wife, the husband must continue to provide the slave-wife with food, clothing, and rights of cohabitation, or she shall go out free. The husband would have to give her a bill of divorce in order to free her for remarriage. He is not permitted to sell her back into slavery or to hold a debt against her. Note the earlier example of Hagar in Genesis 16.

Deuteronomy 21:10-14 protects the rights of a heathen woman taken captive in war. If a man finds a beautiful woman among the captives, he may take her home, shave her head, give her thirty days to mourn her parents, and then marry her. If he finds no delight in her, then he shall let her go free (divorce her). He is not permitted to sell her into slavery because he has dishonored her.

These two instances show that women in that society were at a definite disadvantage in that they could be taken into marriage against their will. They also could be discarded if the husband was not wholly satisfied. If a wife was set aside by a husband without receiving a bill of divorce, then she remained what the Jews called a "chained one" (*egunah*). This meant that the deserted wife would be denied any marital satisfaction or privileges. According to Jewish law, she remained his wife forever, unless he could be found and be persuaded to grant her a *get* (divorce bill).[12]

For this reason, God was compassionate and flexible even though marriage was meant to be indissoluble. Because of the hardness of men's hearts, God gave these rules of divorce so the disadvantaged woman might be set free perhaps to find some man who would have her. God's intention is for marriage to be for life: "Let no one separate" (Matt. 19:6). However, where abuses prevail and marriage ceases to be fulfilling the divine order, God's compassion intervenes. He does not bind these women in marriage for the sake of a legalistic defense of the institution of marriage.

Jesus in presenting the ideal for marriage did not intend to revoke or contradict God's compassionate interest in the abused wife, as shown by these rules. The church should do all that it can to help its people uphold the divine standard for marriage and its ideals, even as many of the rabbis of old endeavored to do. Yet the church will err on the side of legalism if it fails to see the possibility of divine patience with divorce, in its redemptive sense, as a reflection of God's concern for the abused. To allow this does not negate the fact that God hates divorce (Mal. 2:14-16); God hates what men do in putting their wives away for carnal reasons or in inflicting physical and psychological abuse upon them.

Divorce was tolerated if it could alleviate the plight of the wife, who was always at a disadvantage in a patriarchal society which allowed the male almost unlimited abusive powers.

Divorce Forbidden in Certain Circumstances

Just as God was prepared to tolerate divorce to alleviate the bondage of a wife to an uncaring husband, so he was prepared to protect the wife from divorce if she could not protect herself.

If a virgin is raped and she is not betrothed, then she has the option of marrying the rapist, who may not divorce her as long as he lives (Deut. 22:28-29). The Mishnah comments that the ravisher must drink out of his own earthen pot, marry her even if she is lame, blind, or otherwise afflicted.[13] This biblical rule was later modified by rabbinical decisions that would allow him to divorce her if she became an adulteress,[14] or to pay the father fifty shekels in lieu of marriage if the woman has any religious disqualifications.[15]

Divorce was also forbidden under rabbinical law in order to protect those who could not protect themselves. The oral law gives three exceptions to the general privilege of divorce for any cause:

1. If the woman is insane, the scribes of the Mishnah forbid divorce, since the woman is not able to care for herself and could become the prey of evil men.[16] Other rabbis permitted divorce of an insane wife "on the principle that the ancient legal right of the husband could not be abrogated."[17]

2. If a Jewish wife is taken captive in war, a husband can not divorce her while she was in captivity. It is her husband's duty to ransom her, though if captured a second time, he is no longer so obliged.[18]

3. If the wife or betrothed is a minor, she is too young to care for her bill of divorce. A father of the minor who is betrothed or married may accept a divorce for her.[19] If her father died and the minor is given in marriage by her mother or brothers, she may refuse the contract and be set free without need for a bill of divorce.[20]

There is another biblical law which reflects divine concern for the wife. According to Deuteronomy 22:13-21, if a husband lays a charge of premarital incontinence against his wife, the wife's parents are to bring evidence of her virginity, the blood-stained cloth from the marriage bed. If they can do that and thus prove his charge false, he is penalized by having all privileges of divorce taken away from him. If she is guilty as charged, then she is put to death under that early law, and the husband kept the dowry. In order to stop a false accusation by a mercenary hardhearted husband, the law of Deuteronomy 22:19 fined such a husband one hundred shekels of silver to be paid to the bride's father, and his privilege of divorce was revoked. This would make him ponder the risk before making a frivolous charge.

Divine tolerance of divorce in the Old Testament is not a sanction of the patriarchal assumed right to divorce for any cause. Instead, it indulges the long-standing custom in order to bring social benefit to the abused wife. While it was not God's intention that marriages should be broken up, neither was it his will that women should be abused by carnal men.

We may learn from Jesus' teachings on another institution. The Sabbath was made for humankind and not humankind for the Sabbath, meaning that the seventh day should serve the good of people and not be a legal noose around the neck (Mark 2:23-28; 3:1-6). So also marriage was made for human beings, to bring fulfillment to *both* spouses. Where that is not happening, God has shown himself to be more than forgiving and understanding. In this age of so many failing marriages, the church needs to be concerned, courageous, and compassionate in dealing with those who have failed and those who have been abused.

When one comes to the interpretative study of Jesus' statements on divorce, it is important not to forget this positive concern on the part of our merciful God and not to suppose that his Son Jesus is any less compassionate.

Divorce Replaces Stoning for Adultery

The law in Deuteronomy 22:21-22 states that a man or woman guilty of adultery is to be stoned. This was taken literally at the time of the giving of the law. In the time of the monarchy (1000 B.C.), however, we are aware that neither David nor Bathsheba were stoned for their sin. By the time of Jesus (A.D. 30), the death penalty had been practically abolished for adultery.[21] In its place came a ruling of rabbinic law, "A woman who had committed adultery must be divorced."[22]

In the times of the prophets, a husband might pardon his wife for adultery (Hosea), but by the time of Jesus, Jewish law was stricter, and an adulterous wife was forbidden to have intercourse with her husband or adulterer: her husband had to divorce her, as recorded in Sotah 5:1 "As she is forbidden to her husband, she is also forbidden to the adulterer."[23] A further reference to the same law is made by Cohen, "Talmudic law declared that 'a woman who had committed adultery must be divorced.' "[24]

This practice of required divorce, supported by Jewish law, forms part of the background to the interpretation of Jesus' sayings on divorce.

Judicial Separations Required

In the time of Jesus, separations also were required or recommended under certain circumstances: in the event of leprosy[25], or a childless marriage. A Baraita states that if a couple lives childless for ten years, the husband should give his wife a bill of divorce, since the object of marriage had been defeated.[26] The general teaching of the rabbis was that marriage without issue was unholy. Philo of Alexandria (ca. 20 B.C.—A.D. 50) recommends divorce in such cases, lest the gratification of the senses be considered more desirable than progeny.[27] In the time of Abraham the childless marriage was handled by Sarah providing a bond-woman as a second wife or concubine for her husband. The childless Hannah also has to contend with a second wife, Peninnah (1 Sam. 1:1-8).

Wives Could Sue for Divorce

Based on the rules of Exodus 21:7-11, a bondwoman taken as wife could go out free if the husband did not do his duty to her. From this, Jewish legal scholars extrapolated that if a bondwoman had this right, then a free wife under Jewish law could sue, forcing her husband to divorce her, for several reasons: impotence, denial of sexual relationships, forced idleness, suspicion of the husband's intention to desert her, and loathsome ailments or occupations, such as tanning, or collector of dry excrements.[28] He could even be forced to divorce her if she suspected that he was going to move to a foreign land and she preferred to stay in the Holy Land, or the Holy City.[29]

Apostasy from the Jewish faith was another cause for which a wife could appeal to a Jewish court for a divorce bill from her husband.[30] In contrast to this, the apostle Paul recommends that the believer not initiate divorce from an unbelieving spouse (1 Cor. 7:12-16). By A.D. 300 polygamy could be a cause for Jewish divorce, though it was not officially prohibited until about A.D. 1025 by Rabbi Gershom.[31]

Against Divorce for Any Cause

The viewpoint of Hillel, that husbands could divorce for any cause, came under attack by Shammai. Jesus, contemporaneous to both, expresses his opposition to men using their power to divorce for no just cause. By his teaching he makes these men morally responsible for the results of their careless divorces.

Little by little over the next two centuries, other rabbis expressed their views against divorce for any cause: Eleazar (A.D. 80-120), Yohanan (199-279), and Meir (about 150).[32] Amram comments, "The moral sense which condemned the abuse of the right to divorce found its expression in the dicta of Jesus, Eleazar, Yohanan, Meir and Rabha."[33] The rabbis as "practical people" didn't try to prevent divorce for cause or by mutual consent. "They did not foolishly sacrifice the realities of life to the ideal by which they were guided."[34] Eventually, within the rabbis' thinking, the divine intention of the sanctity of the home began to challenge the patriarchal right to divorce for any cause.

Jesus' viewpoint was revolutionary for his age. Radical as his views were, one should not rush to the conclusion that his discourse with the Pharisees was a call for the withdrawal of the divorce privilege in total. It was, however, a judgment upon those who used the bill of divorce as a justification for their right to divorce.

Efforts to Check Divorce

Rabbis did exercise their influence to check the unrestrained passions that often prompted men to divorce. When a man went to the *bet din* (court) to have the divorce bill prepared, the court judges would try to dissuade him by pointing out its effects on the reputation of himself, his wife, and his children.[35] The law also favored remarriage of the divorced couple if the wife had not married another husband after her divorce. Not all rabbis countenanced the abuse of the patriarchal right, but many did, placing the assumed right of the husband above the divine intention for marriage. Jesus was seen by the latter to be challenging a right which they had come to believe was an integral part of Mosaic law. For this, he could be tried for heresy.

The *ketubah* or dowry became one of the most practical checks on divorce. The price was originally paid by the groom to the father (Gen. 24:53; 30:26-43; 34:11-12; Exod. 22:16-17), but in time was given directly to the bride. Since it was still too easy for the husband to tell his wife to take her dowry and go, the law eventually had it given to the bride, but left it undivided from the husband's estate. In the event of divorce, he had to break up his estate and pay her in coin. This would take time and might cause him to rethink his decision to divorce.[36]

Eventually there was a decree by Rabbi Gershom ben Yehudah (ca. A.D. 1025) which said, "As the man does not put away his wife except of his own free will, so shall the woman not be put away except by her own consent."[37] This was applicable only in those cases where neither could show good cause for divorce. It had no application in the time of Jesus, but it does show a growing respect in Jewish law for the position of women.

Status of Divorced Women

Ordinarily a woman was not permitted her own freedom, but according to David Amram the divorced woman became her own mistress.[38] She was neither the property of her husband or her father, and had the right to give herself away in marriage. She could not marry a priest (Lev. 21:7). A priest's daughter who was widowed or divorced could return to her father's house (Lev. 22:12-13), with the right to eat of the offered part of the holy things. Apparently, if there was any social or spiritual stigma to her, it was forgiven. The divorced woman was free to marry whom she desired. According to Jewish law, she could not marry within three months of her divorce in order that there be no doubt of the paternity of any child that she might be carrying.[39]

Conclusions and Questions

Conclusions from this study of Jewish laws on marriage and divorce will aid an interpretation of the sayings of Jesus on the subject. Here are some questions intended to stimulate thought and lead to better understanding of Jesus' words:

1. The original intention of God for marriage, according to Gen. 2:24, was a one-flesh, monogamous, lifelong relationship, intended to fulfill the complementary needs of both male and female. Did Jesus support this intention in his dialogue with the Pharisees? If so, how?

2. In Genesis a joint leadership mandate is given to the man and the woman (1:26). The Fall into sin brings humiliating consequences and God's judgment, and the woman is ruled by the man (3:16). The patriarchal authority which developed was abused by many men from an early time, resulting in the practice of divorce by the husband for any cause. Did Jesus attack the unrestrained abuse of this patriarchal right, especially in the area of divorce? Did he suggest in his sayings that the divorce bill was no excuse for irresponsible divorce or for an acquittal from guilt? Did Jesus object to the husband domineering over his defenseless wife rather than being protective and expressing mutual and complimentary love and respect?

3. The abuse of male leadership led to a double standard of morality: a strict rule against any infidelity on the part of the wife, but a more lenient approach toward the husband's affairs with unattached women. Under rabbinic law a man could be held accountable for committing adultery against another married man (by intercourse with his wife), and a wife was accountable for committing adultery against her husband, but a husband could not be accused of committing adultery against his wife (by intercourse with another woman). Did Jesus attack this double

standard (Matt. 5:27-32; 19:3-12; John 8:1-11)? If so, how?

4. In Old Testament Jewish thinking, divorce concluded marriage and any hold of the former husband over his divorced wife. Since Jewish law stated that a deserted wife remained the wife of the deserting husband forever, the wife could sue him at law to force him to divorce her before or during desertion. Divorce then freed her from a deserting or indifferent husband in order that she might remarry without adultery. Did Jesus really intend to reverse this?

5. The replacing of the death penalty with the required giving of a bill of divorce had become a practice under rabbinical law by the time of Christ. What implications might this have for Jesus' intended meaning of the "except for unchastity" clause in Matthew 19:9? Would Jesus have seen the bill of divorce as a reasonable and more humane substitute to the death penalty?

6. The first commandment, to multiply and fill the earth was important to the Jew. If the death penalty no longer applied to an adulterous wife, then the rabbis reasoned that divorce became an obligation to free the husband to remarry and continue to fulfill that first commandment. In the kingdom of heaven, are some things more important to Jesus that might supersede that first commandment (Matt. 19:12; cf. 1 Cor. 7:7-8, 27)?

7. Does Jesus' attitude of forgiveness give us any lead for a new approach to those guilty of adultery? Might he have encouraged more forgiveness and less divorce? (See Luke 7:37-50; John 8:11; cf. Matt. 1:5-6 and the situation of 1:19-20).

8. Leniency under the Mosaic Law was given to polygamous marriages and some relationships which began with adultery, such as that of David and Bathsheba. Is this indication of grace under law reflected in Jesus' attitude?

3

The Pharisees and Jesus

All four Gospels give evidence of the existing tension between Jesus and at least some of the Pharisees of his day. As we examine this interface of conflict, we will begin to sense what may have been the setting for the statements on divorce by Jesus. This may bring understanding of what he was saying, and perhaps of what he was not saying.

Conflict with the Pharisees

A comparative analysis of the four Gospels on Jesus' interaction with the Pharisees indicates that all are agreed that Jesus was verbally attacked, tested, accused, and endangered by the Pharisees. In turn, all the synoptics (Matthew, Mark, and Luke) demonstrate that Jesus denounced the Pharisees as hypocrites. In John, however, Jesus says they are of their father, the devil. They are called vipers by Jesus in both Matthew and Luke, and they are treated as conceited observers of the law in Luke.

A strong series of woes are pronounced against them by Jesus in Matthew 23 and Luke 11. In Matthew, Jesus accuses them of hypocrisy, binding grievous burdens on others' shoulders without raising a finger to help them, ostentatious works, wearing religious garments to be seen, loving the chief seats, and shutting up the kingdom of heaven to common people. They devour widows' houses, make long pretentious prayers, and pay tithes of garden herbs while omitting the more important matters of the law. They were as whitewashed tombs, clean on the outside and dead on the inside.

Jesus himself is portrayed in the Gospels as a friend of the common people. He associated with the disciples, the poor, the tax collectors, sinners, women such as Mary Magdalene, the woman at the well, and others. This justified the accusations of the Pharisees, that he was a "friend of tax collectors and sinners" (Matt. 11:19). The Pharisees criticized Jesus for healing on the Sabbath, letting his disciples pick grain on the Sabbath, and not insisting on washing hands before eating.

The Pharisees accused him of casting out demons by Beelzebul, called him a liar, and sought to stone, accuse, and arrest him. This conflict forms an important part of the setting for Jesus' sayings on divorce. If we can sense Jesus' concern over the legalistic approach to the law by the Pharisees and especially by the Shammaites, we may not be too quick to read him as agreeing with either Shammai or Hillel.

In Matthew (both 9:13 and 12:7), Jesus quotes Hosea 6:6: "I desire mercy, not sacrifice." Jesus is not a legalist, nor does he appreciate that approach to the interpretation of the law: "Unless your righteousness exceeds that of the scribes and Pharisees, you will never enter the kingdom of heaven" (5:20). With these words Jesus introduces the subject of men being responsible for their adulterous thoughts (5:27-30). Then he questions the right of the husband to put away his wife if she is not guilty of unchastity or adultery. Jesus makes the husband morally responsible for his thoughtless and hard-hearted act (5:31-32).

Development of the Pharisees

The scribes established an order for the purpose of making many Levitical laws of purity universal throughout society. Its members were called *haber* (comrade), but because it made a wall between themselves and other Jews, they were called separatists (Aramaic: *perushim*; Greek: *pharisaioi*; English: *Pharisees*).

They were reputed to be holy ones, separate from the people of the land. Their lay scribes challenged the pretension of the priestly caste to be the sole authoritative interpreter of the Torah. One of the requirements for admission was to be separate from commoners in respect to tithes, heave offerings, and preparation and eating of food.

The Sadducees, opponents of the Pharisees, were identified more with the temple worship. The high priest was a Sadducee and also head of the Sanhedrin, the highest council of the Jews. They accepted only the Old Testament as authoritative in religious and ethical matters.

To the Scriptures the Pharisaic scribes, on the other hand, added oral traditional interpretations (Mark 7:2-8) which were later incorporated in the Mishnah (written about A.D. 200). These "traditions of the elders" they attributed to Moses and thus accorded them divine authority equal to the Torah (Genesis through Deuteronomy). They even began to ascribe greater authority to the words of the scribes than to the written Torah (Matt. 15:1-9). The scribes developed, taught, and administered this oral law.

Rules for interpreting the oral tradition were worked through by Hillel. Different interpretations were maintained by Shammai, his contemporary. The Talmud records some three hundred conflicts between the two. Shammai had a stronger following during the time of Jesus, though Hillel's views came to prevail by the time of the destruction of Jerusalem (A.D. 70). One of their major differences had to do with the right to divorce. Hillel contended that a husband could divorce his wife for any cause; Shammai stipulated divorce for adultery only.

Hillel held that one could keep the Torah in spirit, without as much attention to the detail of the law, while Shammai taught obedience of every detail. Hillel's goal was the same as that of Shammai, the eventual obedience of the tradition of the elders respecting the Torah. But Hillel was more open to proselytes who would attempt to keep the spirit of the law, though failing to understand all of its minutiae.

According to Asher Finkel, Shammai and his disciples at times used force or the threat of it. Zealots among the Shammaites issued measures against any association with the heathen, especially the Syrians and Romans in Galilee.[1] Prior to the destruction of the Temple in A.D. 70, the Shammaite zealots had massacred the Hillelites who opposed the enactment of the Eighteen Measures against the heathen.[2] In the Jamnia academy under Ben Zakkai, well after the fall of Jerusalem, the scholarly efforts of the two academies of Shammai and Hillel were unified, with the decision of Hillel prevailing.

While one cannot state dogmatically that all of Jesus' criticisms of the Pharisees were directed only toward the Shammaites, it is certain that many of them were. Finkel contends that the humbleness, restraint, clear argumentative reasoning, and liberal stand of the Hillelites were close in spirit to that of the teacher of Nazareth.[3]

Traits of the Pharisees

Christian thinking regarding the Pharisees has been colored by their portrayal in the Gospels as rigid legalists with little heart for the common person. Abraham Geiger, a Jewish scholar in Germany, appreciated the Pharisees and some of the Talmudists, especially Hillel and Rabbi Akiba. Geiger tried to divide the Pharisees into two groups. He favored the ones who endeavored to "lighten the burden of the law," such as Hillel, who made some effort to help the common man to understand the "spirit of the law," even though he doubted that they could grasp its details. Rarely was Torah taught to women.[4]

The opposing faction was made up of the "fanatically rigid Sadducees, the Shammaites, and Rabbi Ishmael."[5] The latter represented the "Old Halakah," which Geiger identified as those criticized in the early Christian writings. Louis Finkelstein presents a wealth of material on Pharisaism, but at times in his zeal he seems partial and not as objective as he might be. He contends that Pharisaism became "the foundation for the foremost intellectual and spiritual structure the world has yet seen, Western civilization,"[6] and that it was basic to the rise of both Christianity and Islam.

There is no doubt that Pharisaism as a part of Judaism as a whole did contribute a great deal to the religious world and society in general. Yet this does not erase some of the less-appreciated traits which are well documented, not only in Scripture but in rabbinical writings as well.

Finkelstein does recognize that there were criticisms of the Pharisees by their contemporaries and from within their own parties. He admits that they were guilty of insistence on the mastery and observance of detail in the law, but not of insincerity, fanaticism, and false motives. Yet he says, "Nevertheless, so frequently were these calumnies repeated that they affected the minds of the Pharisees themselves. As their factions parted from one another, each accused the other of vices which the outer world charged against them both."[7]

To substantiate such charges, he quotes a Hillelite who spoke of his Shammaite opponents in terms of treachery, self-pleasers, gluttons, deceitful, and impious: "Do not touch me lest thou shouldst pollute me where I stand."[8] Finkelstein admits that none of the excoriations which Jesus uttered against the whole order could have exceeded this factional denunciation in bitterness by an "observant loyal Pharisee of the gentler group."[9]

From Finkelstein's evidence, it appears that criticisms of the Pharisees were warranted. Consider the seven varieties of Pharisees listed in both the Babylonian and Jerusalem Talmuds: (1) The shoulder Pharisee, who packs his good works on his shoulder to be seen of men. (2) The wait-a-bit Pharisee: when someone wants to do business with him, he says, "Wait a bit, I must do a good work." (3) The reckoning Pharisee, who crosses off a bad work with a good one. (4) The economizing Pharisee, who asks, "What economy can I practice to spare a little for a good work?" (5) The show-me-my-fault Pharisee, who says, "Show me my sin and I will do an equivalent good work. (6) The Pharisee of fear, like Job. (7) The Pharisee of love, like Abraham. This last was the only one dear to God.

The first five demonstrate attitudes that came to be despised by the common man and by many of the Pharisees themselves in due time. The Pharisees had endeavored by teaching and example to establish a higher standard of religion in Judaism. They had gained the reputation of being more religious than their Sadducean opponents or the ignorant and negligent mass of the people.[10] G. F. Moore observes that many sincere Pharisees thought better of themselves in comparison with others than is good, and that these superior airs were often quite disagreeable.

A great bitterness developed on the part of the common folk against the more cultured who lived in Jerusalem. Rabbi Eleazar remarked, "If the *'am ha-arets* [people of the land] did not need us for the purpose of trade, they would slaughter us."[11] Finkelstein points out that the common farmer, the simple and naive, were not given any helpful attention by the priesthood and "were ready to receive the imprint of the first teacher who ministered to them."[12]If the priesthood felt it beneath them to bother with the *'am ha-arets,* so did the Shammaites. The Hillelites were more open to them, willing to assist them to try to observe the Torah so that they might gradually understand it and obey it.

Thus it is no wonder that, when Jesus came bringing the gospel to the poor (Luke 4:18), the crowds began to follow him. His disciples were chosen from among the *'am ha-arets,* and Jesus ministered without airs among them, healing their sick and teaching them with illustrations easily understood. He also questioned a piety linked to a form of legalism, though he upheld the spirit of the Mosaic Law without bondage to its letter. He labeled hypocrisy among the religious leaders of the day. That delighted the crowd that followed him, but angered those same leaders. When Jesus befriended the common folk, he set the stage for becoming an enemy of the Pharisees and of the aristocracy of Jerusalem.

Jesus' Criticisms of the Pharisees

Most of Jesus' criticisms were likely directed at the more dominant group, the Shammaites. In Matthew, Jesus ridicules their enforcement of the elaborate details of the law. He says that they "strain out a gnat but swallow a camel" (23:24) and "tie up heavy burdens, hard to bear, and lay them on the shoulders of others" (23:4). Shammai's separation was such that he and his followers best fit Jesus' words, "Woe to you, scribes and Pharisees, hypocrites! For you lock people out of the kingdom of heaven. For you do not go in yourselves, and when others are going in, you stop them" (23:13).

Asher Finkel demonstrates that the woes Jesus pronounces against the Pharisees in Matthew 23:2-35 apply only to the Pharisaic Shammaites:

1. "You shut up the kingdom of heaven against men." The Shammaites classified candidates for the "world to come" into three categories, one of which was reproaches and everlasting abhorrence, to which the sinners were assigned. To the Shammaites, these sinners were beyond the understanding of the law, so no effort was made to reach them. In fact, they did their best to have no contact with them, lest they be polluted.

2. "You compass land and sea to make one proselyte. . . ." In accepting converts, Shammaites were very strict, requiring those circumcised prior to conversion (e.g., Arabs) to submit to the drawing of blood, while the Hillelites did not. The Shammaites made conversion difficult.

3. "You blind guides which say whosoever shall swear by the Temple it is nothing, but whosoever shall swear by the gold of the temple, he is debtor!" cf. Mark 7:10-11. On regulations governing the declaration of vows the Shammaites were very strict, while the Hillelites were more lenient.

4. "You tithe mint, dill, cummin and every herb and have neglected the weightier matters of the law." The Shammaites were stricter in their requirements than the Hillelites, requiring a tithe of herbs and vegetables.

5. "You declare a state of purity for the outside of a cup and the platter, but within they are full of rapacity and wantonness." The school of Shammai held that "first one washes the hands and then fills the cup" while the school of Hillel allowed the reverse. Shammai obviously felt that there was a state of purity to the outside of the cup requiring washed hands.

6. In Matthew 23:5 Jesus attacks the enlarging of the fringes of their garments as being ostentatious. The Shammaites required fringes of four fingers length with four twisted cords at the corners, while the Hillelites only required three.

7. "You are the children of them which killed the prophets. . . ." Jesus identifies force and violence with the Pharisees. This fits the spirit of Shammai more so than the gentle-spirited Hillel. As noted above the Shammaite zealots had massacred the Hillelites who opposed the enactment of the Eighteen Measures against the heathen.[13]

Conclusions and Questions

The following conclusions need to be carried forward into any effort to understand what Jesus was saying in his discussion of divorce with the Pharisees. Was he aligning himself with Shammai, who was so rigid and legalistic and probably his bitterest enemy? Or with Hillel, who held that husbands could divorce for any cause? Or with neither?

1. There is ample evidence that Jesus was in conflict with the Pharisees, and especially with Shammai and his followers.

2. A fault of the Pharisees lay in too much emphasis on the letter of the law, including the oral tradition, which was not part of the original Torah. Jesus criticized them for extreme legalism.

3. The Pharisees on the whole, but especially the Shammaites, were not friendly toward common persons (*'am ha-arets*, people of the land). These common people did not appreciate the attitudes of at least some of the Pharisees. In contrast, Jesus made a point of going to the poor and the sinners. He tells the Pharisees that the sick need the physician (Matt. 9:12).

4. Jesus' popularity with the *'am ha-arets* made him unpopular with the scribes and Pharisees.

5. There are good grounds for differentiating between various types of Pharisees. On the basis of Jewish sources, some were violently opposed to any who differed with their interpretation of the law. Many were branded hypocritical by other types of Pharisees. The Shammaites of Jesus' day would appear best to fit this description.

6. Jesus was inclined to see things as did Hillel, who was more liberal in his acceptance of the *'am ha-arets*. He obviously differed with Hillel on divorce for any cause, but even more vociferously with the followers of Shammai in general.

7. While Shammai appeared more rigid than Hillel, it should be remembered that both were Pharisees whose chief goal was to bring universal obedience to the law by all Jews, by the observance of the laws of purity and all which that entailed. The net result was a system in which works of obedience to the oral traditions tended to overwhelm or distract from a true experience of God's grace and forgiveness.

4

Jesus, the Model of Caring for Sinners

Our goal is to interpret Jesus' sayings regarding divorce with as much accuracy as possible. To do so, we need to examine the attitudes Jesus demonstrated in his interaction with those who failed to keep the high ideals he taught for marriage. There is a clear contrast between his attitude toward "sinners" and those who are the custodians of the law. He is so openly receptive to common sinners, while apparently despising the manner in which the scribes and Pharisees apply the law to life's situations.

Challenging Hypocrites

Harshness in Jesus' attitude is reserved for those who are hypocritical in respect to the law. Jesus speaks to the scribes and Pharisees: "You hypocrites! . . . 'This people honors me with their lips, but their hearts are far from me; in vain do they worship me, teaching human precepts as doctrines' " (Matt. 15:7-9).

The self-righteous attitudes of these religious leaders calls forth Jesus' reproach because through their study of the Scriptures, they should know better. They neglect the weightier matters of the covenant law, justice, mercy, and faith. In addition, their teaching roles give them opportunity to mislead others regarding what is of most importance in the service of God.

Hypocrites appears like a refrain in Matthew 23. The scribes and Pharisees are "blind guides" and full of "hypocrisy and lawlessness." The three synoptic Gospels are united in their witness that Jesus attacked hypocrisy among the religious leaders, and especially among the scribes and Pharisees.[1] Jesus exhorted his followers to live in a different way (Matt. 23:3; 8-12). Therefore, we are called to self-examination as we learn from our one instructor, the Messiah (23:10).

Befriending Sinners

In contrast to Jesus' attitude toward hypocrites, he reaches out to common sinners, demonstrating an understanding of their struggles. He does not condone their sin, but neither does he approach them in a judgmental manner. His opponents criticize him as a friend of sinners.[2] The Pharisees are hesitant to eat with the common people, lest they be contaminated. But Jesus does so in a public manner that irritates the Pharisees. He identifies with sinners with a purpose to lift them: "Those who are well have no need of a physician, but those who are sick" (Matt. 9:12). He justifies this association with sinners on the grounds of mercy, not sacramental holiness, by quoting Hosea 6:6, "I desire mercy, not sacrifice."

If Jesus can associate with sinners without condoning their sin, then may not the church follow his model? This compassionate approach of Jesus has a strong theological foundation in both the incarnation and the cross, in which Jesus identifies with us in our temptations and our sins. He "came to seek out and to save the lost" (Luke 19:10).

Jesus shows respect for the dignity and worth of common sinners. We see this as he converses with the woman at the well in Samaria, despite her five previous marriages and her current common-law situation. And later, as he invites himself to the house of Zacchaeus, the despised tax collector. Jesus does not condemn these two but offers them grace and salvation. The reputation of Mary Magdalene, out of whom Jesus casts seven demons (Luke 8:2-3) could cause some consternation but Jesus, undeterred, accepts her ministry. She has been honored through the centuries as the first witness of the resurrected Lord (John 20:1, 16).

Two other incidents clearly show that Jesus' relationship to common sinners is not on a legalistic basis. While Jesus eats in the house of a Pharisee (Luke 7:36-50), "A woman . . . who was a sinner" comes in. For some time she weeps over Jesus' feet, kissing them, and bathing them with her tears. She dries his feet with her hair and then anoints them with ointment. Simon the Pharisee questions in his heart the wisdom of Jesus and doubts that he is a prophet. Jesus rebuffs him, preferring to identify with the repentant woman of sin, whom he sends away forgiven.

A somewhat similar incident is recorded in John 8:3-11. A woman caught in adultery is brought before Jesus by the scribes and the Pharisees, to test him on Moses' law on stoning.[3] There are several significant features here:

1. Only the woman is brought. The double standard is obvious. Where is the man who was also involved "in the very act"? This clearly demonstrates the abuse of the patriarchal right of the male.

2. Jesus' statement pinpoints the sinful nature of the Pharisees and of men in general: "Let anyone among you who is without sin be the first to throw a stone at her."

3. In the tradition of the elders, stoning was replaced by a required bill of divorce. So it is likely that the Pharisees are attempting to impale Jesus on either the horn of the Mosaic Law or on the horn of the Oral Tradition.

4. Jesus obviously abhors the injustice in the case.

5. He is sensitive to the embarrassment of the woman and refuses to bring condemnation upon her.

In these accounts, one can see that Jesus refuses to be embarrassed or intimidated by the sinful reputations of those to whom he ministers as a friend. Neither the opinions of the legalistic Pharisees nor the letter of the law can deter Jesus' concern for sinners. He sees the need of the individual, and with little mention of one's past failings, he associates with that one in an open receptivity. He recognizes humanity's sin and is gracious toward sinners.

Applying Law to Life in a Nonlegalist Manner

If we ponder Jesus' attitude in the above incidents, it becomes difficult to suppose that, in his discussion on divorce with the Pharisees, he would apply Mosaic Law in a heartless or legalistic manner. In the antitheses in Matthew 5:17-48, Jesus contrasts the letter of the law with the spirit of the law and calls us to fulfill the spirit of the law. Yet in dealing with sinners, Jesus displays God's grace toward those who show any inclination toward repentance or a searching for the truth. He calls us higher than the letter of the law, but judges us with grace. In dealing with the Samaritan woman and with the woman caught in the act of adultery, he applies the law with grace and patience toward those who most needed his help.

Insight regarding Jesus' application of law to life may be seen in his treatment of the Sabbath. Jesus allows hungry disciples to pick grain on the Sabbath (Mark 2:23-28) and defends the right to heal on the Sabbath (John 5:9-18; 7:23; Matthew 12:9-13), despite the criticism of the Pharisees. Jesus teaches that Sabbath observance need not be threatened by a compassionate interpretation of its purpose, which was for the good of humankind and not just as an end in itself.

Under the law one may not work, light fires, or gather sticks for a fire without threat of the death penalty. In Numbers 15:32-36, a man is stoned for gathering sticks on the Sabbath. But according to Jesus, the Sabbath was made for the welfare of people and not the reverse. Jesus applies the principle that the institution of the Sabbath was for the good of humanity, in opposition to the letter of the law (Exod. 31:13-15). Is it not also reasonable to recognize that the institution of marriage, like the Sabbath, is for the good of humanity? Marriage is to serve the needs of God's highest creation, even those who don't use it properly the first time, and not to be an end in itself.

This does not mean that partners should take their marriage vows lightly. Likewise, it can not be said that Jesus did away with the Sabbath principle because he engaged in some compassionate exceptions. The marriage covenant is to be taken seriously, and so is the Sabbath principle. Note well what is observed from the study of Jesus' relationship to sinners and the law. He does not allow the letter of the law to interfere with his compassionate efforts to minister to those who have failed under that law. This must be borne in mind as one seeks to interpret Jesus on divorce.

In a Jewish Setting, According to Matthew

Mark and Luke both differ from each other in the divorce passages, and each of these is different again from Matthew's account. These variations can be explained in part by the purpose of the author and his intended readers. Matthew wrote for a Jewish audience. Both Luke and Mark slanted their writing toward the Gentiles, resulting in accounts that don't always give attention to what Jesus may have been facing within the Jewish context.

Some scholars have made a serious study of the sources used in the writing of the synoptic Gospels. They disagree as to which Gospel should be taken as the primary source for the divorce passages.

For a thorough review of the problem by a conservative scholar, see Donald Guthrie's *New Testament Introduction*.[4] Werner Kümmel, a more liberal scholar, gives an adequate summary of the history of the synoptic problem in his *Introduction to the New Testament*.[5] Scholars like Kümmel, Taylor, Orlinski, Klostermann, W. C. Allen, Albright, and Mann tend to support the primacy of Mark's account over that of Matthew.[6] Most of these interpret the phrases *for any cause* and *except for fornication* in Matthew 19:3 and 9 as editorial insertions placed in the text to reflect the discussion current in the time of Jesus between the two schools of Pharisees led by the strict Shammai and the more liberal Hillel.[7] There is not sufficient reason for adopting this viewpoint.

A number of able scholars support the primacy of Matthew's divorce passage (19:3-9) over Mark's (10:2-12), believing that it better represents the actual historical setting in its Jewish context. Orlinski cites Merx and Muller as agreeing that Matthew is the best source for this Gospel account.[8] Anderson favors Matthew as primary and, like Nineham, feels that no Jew, let alone a Pharisee would have put the question to Jesus as in Mark 10:2, whereas the question in Matthew 19:3 is a reference to an actual question debated by the Pharisees.[9] Rist holds that neither Gospel depends on the other, but that both are dependent on strong oral tradition.[10]

Opinions among the church fathers lean toward the primacy of Matthew's Gospel in general over that of Mark's. Augustine supposed Mark to be a condensation of Matthew, while Irenaeus, Clement of Alexandria, and Origen, but not Papias, suggest that Matthew was earlier than Mark.[11]

Farmer contends that Matthew is prior to Mark.[12] Both Butler and the French scholar Vaganay believed that Mark's account was dependent on a Greek Matthew derived from the Aramaic Matthew.[13] Abel Isaksson argues for the primacy of Matthew. He cites J. Schmid as saying that in Mark the "saying of Jesus had been adapted to the conditions in a non-Jewish Christian Milieu."[14] Isaksson holds that Matthew's divorce account is fully consistent with the contemporary Jewish environment. Schmid considers Matthew's account, while dependent on Mark, to be more logically constructed, to be more Jewish, and therefore probably to reproduce the original controversy between Jesus and his opponents in a more accurate fashion. Rudolf Bultmann appears to concur: "Matthew has carried out his revision in an outstanding fashion. . . . Through his emendations Matthew has come closer to the historical truth."[15]

Those of us with a conservative outlook regard Bultmann as a radical. This makes his assessment all the more interesting. In his commentary on B. F. Streeter's exposition, he comments on the improved account in Matthew: "It is quite sufficient to assume that Matthew has made some excellent emendations to the account in Mark."[16]

B. F. Streeter has done a monumental study in *The Four Gospels: A Study of Origins*. He contends for the general priority of Mark over Matthew and Luke, yet he holds that Matthew's divorce passage (19:3-12) along with two others (15:22-28; 12:9-13) in certain respects appear to be closer to the original than that in Mark. He considers that Matthew had an older Palestinian source (M), that Matthew's passage is given in a more natural manner, and that it is more true to contemporary life.[17]

Streeter gives four reasons for giving the divorce passage in

Matthew 19 priority over that of Mark 10:

1. *For every cause* in verse 3 reflects the current debate between Hillel's and Shammai's followers.

2. Our Lord's reply regarding Genesis in verse 6, "They are no longer two, but one flesh," is also a natural response for him.

3. The reference to the law of divorce in verse 7 in Matthew comes more appropriately in the Pharisees' reply than in Mark (10:3) portraying it as our Lord's original question to the Pharisees.

4. Finally, Matthew's arrangement makes more effective his final rejoinder in 19:11-12, that this was merely permissive.

After examining the records of the Gospels and the varying opinions of scholars, the writer has reached the conclusion that Matthew gives us the history most suited to the actual Jewish situation in Jesus' ministry. Matthew's account takes in Jesus' obvious differences with the Pharisees, as well as the debate raging in Jesus' time between the two houses (schools) of the Pharisees, Shammai and Hillel: does a man have the power and legal right to divorce his wife "for any cause"?

Matthew's account presents the spirit of Jesus' teaching within the framework of his opposition to a form of legalism that emphasizes external piety and tends to excuse the abuse of the woman on the basis of a badly interpreted law in Deuteronomy 24.[18] If we explore this story in its primary setting in Matthew, we will be better prepared to catch the spirit of Jesus in applying his commands and his mercy in the church today.

5

Matthew 5 as Context for Matthew 19

Jesus, in Matthew 5:17-20, reveals that he did not come to do away with the old law, nor to bring in a new law, but to uncover the intent of the old law and to bring it to its fullest expression. The antitheses ("It was said. . . . But I say to you. . . .") of 5:21-48 complement and illustrate what Jesus was saying.

In verse 19, Jesus suggests that the scribes and Pharisees have relaxed the proper teaching of the spirit of the law and have ceased to be good examples for those they teach: "Unless your righteousness exceeds that of the scribes and Pharisees, you will never enter the kingdom of heaven." Such direct criticism of the Pharisees no doubt led to their open attack upon the teacher from Galilee, as shown in Matthew 19:3-12.

Jesus upholds a high standard for marriage, based on God's intention, as expressed in Genesis 2:24. In so doing he questions the right of the male to his lustful thoughts (Matthew 5:28) and to his patriarchal right to divorce his wife (19:3-12; 5:32) without just cause. Both the scribes and the Pharisees pride themselves on their knowledge and interpretation of the law. Yet it is precisely their failure to grasp the spirit of the law, despite their attention to its letter, that Jesus is exposing. His rebuke is illustrated in the examples given in the contrasts of the antitheses in 5:21-48.

The Significance of the Antitheses

In Matthew 5:17-20, Jesus indicates that he came to fulfill the law, that is, to reveal its full meaning, and to fulfill its prophetic elements. In this context he is not interested in its prophetic elements as much as in the full revelation of the meaning and intent of the law. He emphasizes the importance of teaching these laws and encouraging obedience to them, but not in the spirit of pride and legalism which he has noticed in the scribes and Pharisees. True righteousness involves obedience, not just to the letter, but to the spirit of the law out of love for God.

This emphatic point is important because it forms the background and context for the later encounter of the Pharisees with Jesus in Matthew 19:3-12. Jesus' verbal assault on the Pharisees and scribes contrasts their righteousness with that which is needed for entrance into the kingdom of heaven: "Unless your righteousness exceeds that of the scribes and Pharisees, you will never enter the kingdom of heaven" (5:20). He proceeds to demonstrate that any who keep only the letter of the law and fail to fulfill the spirit of the law fall far short of the demand of the covenant law of love.

Jesus' radical statements in the antitheses are not to be understood as a new law, nor as a doing away of the old. Instead, it is an indication of the calling of God in the lives of his people to live on the highest plain possible through a sensitivity to the will of God as revealed in the law.

The motive for obedience to the spirit of the law should not be from pride nor from any desire to be seen of men. Jesus attacks the ostentatious tendencies common in the religious leadership of his time in Matthew 6:1-7, 16: "Beware of practicing your piety before others in order to be seen by them. . . . Do not let your left hand know what your right hand is doing. . . . Whenever you pray, go into your room and shut the door. . . . Whenever you fast, do not look dismal, like the hypocrites . . . to show others. . . ."

Many of the Pharisees did fit the above description and were reproached by some of their own for such "holy grandstanding." They no doubt smarted under such open criticism, besides being angered that this Galilean should question their traditional interpretations of the law before such crowds of common sinners.

In Matthew 5, Jesus radicalizes the law in the matters of (1) anger against one's brother, (2) looking with lust at a woman, (3) divorcing one's wife, (4) making oaths, (5) retaliation against wrongs done to oneself, and (6) hating one's enemies.

The strength of fulfilling such demands as turning the other cheek (5:39) and loving the enemy (5:44) are to be derived from one's commitment to love God and neighbor, and not simply from the fact that the law is better explained. It is not a heightened legalism, such as Shammai called for, that Jesus is presenting, but a call to enter into the new covenant life of the Spirit. The prophet Jeremiah (31:33) records God's promise that he would write his laws in the fleshy tables of the heart. The writer to the Hebrews (8:10) gives it application to the age of grace under the new covenant. And Jesus says, "No one can see [understand] the kingdom of God without being born from above" (John 3:3).

In Jesus' radical statements on adultery (v. 28) and divorce (v. 32), he is actually attacking the patriarchal right of the male to have a double standard in marriage. That ancient standard permitted him lustful activity and divorce without good cause. When the Pharisees come and test Jesus on the subject of divorce (Matt. 19:3-9), the basic question is really that of the age-old patriarchal right of the male. They feel this is well established in the law of Moses, and they think they really have Jesus up against their supreme authority. At least, they seek to embroil him in the current controversy between the strict Shammai and the more liberal Hillel on the question of the husband's right to divorce for "any cause."[1]

The church of the Western world, as led by Rome and later by the Reformers, has for centuries applied the words of Jesus on divorce and remarriage with a legalistic zeal. This heavy judgmental and disciplinarian approach toward those divorced is in the spirit of Shammai, one of Jesus' strongest opponents. If the church today can see this, it can minister with compassion to the failing as Jesus did, without giving up Jesus' high standard for marriage. He is our best model for making this a reality. It is the contention of this study that Jesus never meant his words to be applied with any kind of legalism, but as a call to all humanity to walk the high road of obedience in fidelity and love.

In fairness, it should be noted that eventually Pharisees of a later time observed the more compassionate approach of Jesus.

A Comparison of Shammai, Hillel, and Jesus

Shammai, a leader of the more rigid school of Pharisees, was actually more powerful during Jesus' time than was his contemporary, Hillel. The Hillelites came to prevail after the fall of Jerusalem in A.D. 70. Regarding divorce, Shammai taught that adultery or some sexually immoral indiscretion was the only interpretation of "unseemly thing" in Deuteronomy 24:1 and therefore the only justification for divorce by law. Hillel taught that divorce could be for "any cause."

Hillel sought to establish a harmony between Scripture and oral tradition, to prove that what was explicit in tradition was implicit in Scripture. He also recognized that rules must take account of the actual conditions of life. With respect to marriage, he taught that if a man had to be held in an unpleasant marriage against his will, it was short of the ideal for marriage. His interpretation of Deuteronomy 24:1-4 was consistent with this position: if a man finds some unpleasantness in his wife, then he may divorce her.

Hillel's understanding of the patriarchal right of the husband to have power over his wife was basic to his interpretation. That same kind of thinking had led to many abuses over the years against wives and contributed to a low view of marital love and fidelity. Jesus reacts strongly against this view when he reaffirms the divine intention for marriage: A man should leave his father and mother and cleave to his wife in a one-flesh relationship. "Let no one separate" them. In the Jewish context, this was directed to the males because they were the only ones who were allowed to divorce the partner (Matt. 19:5-6). And we recognized that in other settings, it is a command to be received by everyone.

Shammai contended that the "objectionable" or "unseemly thing" of Deuteronomy 24:1 referred to adultery and was the only basis for divorce. At first glance it would appear that Jesus is in agreement with Shammai. In Matthew 5:32 and 19:9, the "except for unchastity" clause could be interpreted to mean divorce only in the case of the wife's adultery. This view is to be rejected.

There are several good reasons to hold that Jesus did not propose this kind of legalism:

1. Unless there is clear contrary evidence, Jesus' conflict with the Pharisees and with Shammai in particular implies in general that it is unlikely that he would support Shammai's position.

2. Jesus repeatedly attacked the rigid legalism of Shammai, so indifferent to the needs of the *'am ha-arets*, the people of the land who do not keep the oral law, common sinners. Jesus was a friend of sinners, one who understood their propensity to sin and sought to lead them to higher ground. So why would he side with those who come to attack him in Matthew 19:3, testing his earlier stated views (Matt. 5:28, 32)?

3. Remember that Jesus sided with mercy over legalism in Matthew 9:13 and 12:7, when he quoted Hosea 6:6, "I desire mercy, not sacrifice." Jesus rejected the binding of grievous burdens on others' shoulders for the sake of external piety (Matt. 23:4).

4. Jesus was concerned about the abuse of the patriarchal right of the husband over his wife in this matter of divorce. The excepting clause is not intended to give a reason for divorce. Instead, it limits the guilt of the male when the wife has already been guilty of unchastity. The husband does not cause her to commit adultery if she is already so involved (Matt. 5:32).

5. The rabbinical law of Jesus' time required divorce in the event of adultery. The excepting clause could be considered to be nothing more than a restatement of this principle. But then, why state the obvious unless there was another point that Jesus was making? That point was to emphasize the guilt of the male who abused his right of authority over his wife.

6. It has already been established earlier in this study that the passage in Deuteronomy 24:1-4 was not a law requiring that a bill of divorce be given. Instead, it regulated the current custom

of the divorce bill and restrained a man from returning to his first wife after divorcing her and marrying another. In Matthew 19:4-6 Jesus completely bypasses any reference to the Deuteronomy passage and goes to God's highest standard for marriage. He is really not interested in exceptions as a legalistic reason for divorce.

Shammai disdained the common folk (*'am ha-arets*) and considered them to be almost unable to understand or obey the law. Hillel was willing to help them take the first step if they had good intentions. Solomon Zeitlin recalls an anecdote where a heathen asked Shammai if he could be converted, but first requested that he be instructed in the entire Torah while he stood on one foot. Shammai ordered him away. He then took the same request to Hillel, who replied, "What is hateful to you, do not to your fellowman. This is the entire Torah and the rest is commentary: go and study."[2]

Jesus goes further in that he summarized the law in a simple, positive statement from Scriptures: "Love God and your neighbor as yourself" (from Matt. 22:36-39; Deut. 6:5; Lev. 19:18). Jesus reveals that faith could bring Jew and non-Jew alike unto the reality of God, and the details of the oral law were inconsequential when they conflicted with God's mercy. It is obvious that, in his attitude toward the *'am ha-arets*, Hillel is much closer to Jesus than is Shammai.

Zeitlin felt that Hillel was a realist who knew human nature: Don't injure your fellow, if you don't want to be injured. In his interpretation, the law is based on self-love. Zeitlin thinks that Jesus' statement, "Love your enemies," was humanly impossible. In response to this we see Jesus, who loved with a self-giving love, even unto death. For humanity to fulfill this kind of love requires the life of the Holy Spirit under the new covenant, where God's law is written on the fleshy tables of the heart.

To follow Zeitlin's line of thought, Hillel was only looking for that which was humanly possible, born of self-love. Consequently, divorce was the expected thing, justified by a wrong and self-indulgent interpretation of Deuteronomy 24:1-4 which was based on an abuse of the patriarchal right of the husband.

Shammai, the legalist, more willing than Hillel to bend life to fit his interpretation of the law, tried to bind people to his ruling and limit divorces to adulterous causes only. Thus he forced divorce on those who were guilty of adultery, without room for forgiveness.

Summary

Jesus rejected the approaches of both Shammai and Hillel. Instead, he issued a call, a divine imperative upon the consciences of all men to accept the divine intention for marriage, to honor a lifelong commitment in love, to uphold fidelity of husband to wife and wife to husband, and to have a forgiving spirit (John 8:11; cf. Hos. 2—3). In making this call to conscience, Jesus did not do away with the provision of the divorce bill, or remarriage, where both might be needed in the face of the hard-heartedness of some of humanity. He did not call for an enforced celibacy following divorce. But Jesus did bring his hearers to face the responsibilities and guilt that befall those who divorce for the wrong reasons.

6

Matthew 5:27-32

In the light of evidence from the Jewish laws on patriarchal rights, marriage, divorce, and from the tension and conflict between Jesus and the Pharisees, one is inclined to take Jesus' statements on divorce as gospel, that is, good news for the good of humanity. They are not a model for the civil regulation of marriage, but a call to discipleship. Failure under this call is forgivable because the gospel, including the law, is of grace.

The Antitheses

The antitheses of Matthew 5 serve to illuminate depths and implications in the law, while revealing the potential failure of any legalistic approach toward the law. The Pharisees are illustrative, at least at times, of failure to follow the spirit of the law. Because Jesus rebukes them for this, their question to test him in Matthew 19 is countering his teaching in Matthew 5:17-48.[1] Jesus says, "You have heard that it was said, 'You shall not commit adultery.' But I say to you that everyone who looks at a woman with lust has already committed adultery with her in his heart" (5:27-28).

Jesus makes a radical application of the divine intention for faithfulness in marriage by taking what he knows to be a fairly common experience to men. He suggests that a man who harbors lustful thoughts toward one not his spouse adulterates his marital relationship by detracting from the "cleaving" principle (Gen. 2:24, KJV). If a man is truly to cleave to his wife for his sexual, social, and spiritual satisfaction, then there is no place for illicit sexual fantasy.

As in each of the antitheses, Jesus is not proposing something that is easy to attain. They must therefore not be taken as heightened legalisms, but as a call to a higher plane of living. At this level of righteousness, Jesus could say, "Let him who is without sin cast the first stone" (based on John 8:7).

In the next antithesis, Jesus recites, "It was also said, 'Whoever divorces his wife, let him give her a certificate of divorce'" (5:31).[2]

The New Revised Standard Version has caught the sense of continuity between verses 27-30 and 31 by the use of the word *also*. One could paraphrase: "While I'm on the topic of adultery, what about those men who put away their wife with the excuse of a divorce bill?"

Irresponsible Divorce

In this passage Jesus is not as concerned about a man divorcing an unfaithful spouse as he is with irresponsible divorce because of the selfishness of the male. He challenges the previously undisputed power of the husband's patriarchal right.

"Let him give her . . ." is a command in the aorist imperative. Jesus here draws attention to the misunderstanding of the law in Deuteronomy 24:1. In the thinking of Hillel and others who preceded him, Moses commanded the giving of a divorce bill if the husband found some unpleasantness in his wife. Jesus' antithesis suggests that he takes exception to this interpretation: "But I say to you that anyone who divorces his wife, except on the ground of unchastity, causes her to commit adultery; and whoever marries a divorced woman commits adultery" (Matt. 5:32).

Compare the Revised Standard Version for part of this verse: the man who divorces his wife "makes her an adulteress." Frank Stagg[3] writes that the divorced woman is "made adulterous" or "victimized with respect to adultery." Her social standing is that of an adulteress. In any case the man stands guilty unless the wife herself has been personally guilty of adultery. If the latter were the case, then the current law in Jesus' time would require that the woman be divorced in lieu of stoning.

Jesus here repudiates the misunderstanding which had catered to the whims of the husbands on the basis of their patriarchal right and a badly interpreted law (Deut. 24:1-4). He calls for them to think seriously about the implications of their actions in divorcing without good cause.

Despite their traditional right, they could be guilty of forcing or entrapping the wife who is the victim of divorce into a second marriage for economic survival and companionship. This would adulterate God's high intention for the first marriage. Men could also be involved in an adulterating act by marrying a wife who had been divorced. Jesus well understands that divorce frees the woman to remarry. This was the custom in Greek, Roman, and Jewish civil law. But Jesus is determined to point out that those who act irresponsibly in divorcing their wives fail under the spirit of the law; their righteousness falls short (Matt. 5:20).

The husband who divorces an innocent wife stands guilty under the spirit of the law because he creates the situation of his wife's remarriage by his action in divorcing her. He stigmatizes her as adulterous, having treated her as he would have treated an adulteress.

The Excepting Clause

"Except on the ground of unchastity" or "except for marital unfaithfulness" (Matt. 5:32, NIV) has adequate textual support. Some scholars such as Kümmel, Brunner, and Montefiore think this phrase might be an interpolation (editorial insertion) that Matthew added into the text as an accommodation to the Shammaites. It has already been shown that Jesus had little appreciation of the Shammaite interpretation of the law, so it is unlikely that either he or his disciples would have endeavored to align themselves with Shammai.

Montefiore thinks that the clause only brings out the original meaning: "For it may be argued that adultery on the woman's

part, of itself, dissolved the marriage." He feels the editor or re-
dactor brought in the clause to soften the uncompromising uni-
versality of the denunciation.

> The extreme attitude, possibly taken up by Jesus, that under no
> circumstances is divorce permissible, is untenable and objection-
> able; but the implied attack upon the inferiority of women in Ori-
> ental society, and upon the unjust power of divorce given to men,
> was of the highest importance and value.[4]

Stagg agrees with Montefiore's last point: "What Jesus said
may best be understood against the background of a man-
centered world in which a husband could boast that in giving a
rejected wife a bill of divorce he protected her rights."[5] Jesus was
certainly against any self-righteous attitudes on the part of the
husband when it came to a broken marriage. Bruce Vawter, the
Roman Catholic scholar, thinks that Matthew adapted the Lord's
saying by the addition of the "except" clause to fit the standards
of a society where fornication had long been regarded as making
divorce mandatory.[6]

There is no need to suppose a redaction[7] or later interpolation
to explain the excepting clause. It is not in the accounts in either
Mark or Luke simply because they tended to treat their material
for their specific Gentile audience. The three Gospels are agreed
that Jesus holds a high standard for marriage, and does not take
lightly the matter of divorce. The excepting clause merely states
the obvious, that the wife when guilty of adultery is responsible
for her own ruin. If the wife by her unfaithful conduct has made
the marriage impossible and the husband is legally forced to divorce her, then he is not open to criticism.[8] This clause also
makes clear Jesus' chief point for the divorcing couple: *If the wife
is not guilty, then the husband is.* It simply qualifies his attack
against the abuse of the traditional male right to divorce.

Remarriage

Jesus also declares, "Whoever marries a divorced woman
commits adultery" (Matt. 5:32). The subjunctive mood in the
verb *marries* suggests that it is probable that the divorced wife
will remarry. The second husband becomes party to the first

husband's sin by marrying his divorced wife. He does not cause the divorce, neither does Jesus suggest that he contributes to the problems of the first marriage. The first husband carries the blame for this adulterating of the second husband because the second marriage adulterates God's intention for the first marriage.

Commits adultery is in the present and suggests that the individual is involved in an adulteration that has a long-lasting effect. This durative sense need not be taken to mean that within a second marriage every sexual act is an occasion for adultery. It is best to simply recognize that the first marriage was once for all adulterated by the second.

Divorce in itself adulterates God's intention for marriage in a legal way, and now the second marriage completes that adulteration in a physical way. As with many things in this less-than-ideal world, the grace of God cleanses us who repent from all sins, from all life lived below the ideal. Second marriages can be blessed of God, because he is gracious. Jesus did not intend to say otherwise even as he put the legalistic approach to the law into proper perspective.

Conclusions and Applications

In summarizing Jesus' sayings on divorce in Matthew 5, several factors demonstrate that Jesus is not stating an outright legalistic prohibition of divorce and remarriage. Instead, he is giving a clearer sense of God's will respecting marriage and the practice of divorce. He is calling all true disciples to the higher righteousness of the kingdom of heaven.

1. The divorce bill under the law is seen to be a protection for the wife against the hard-heartedness of her husband.

2. Remarriage of the wife is possible as part of that provision and is not directly challenged by Jesus.

3. The excepting clause makes clear that Jesus is not ruling out the possibility that a husband victimized by an adulterous wife may remarry without bearing the guilt of adulterating his first marriage since she had already done so.

4. Under the Mosaic law, the adulterous wife was to have been put to death; that then would free the husband from her adul-

tery. In the time of Christ, in lieu of death, divorce was required, so that the husband was free for remarriage.

5. Those of the school of Hillel allowed divorce for "any cause." Jesus speaks clearly against this. He opposes the irresponsible use of the patriarchal right in divorce.

6. Jesus reacts against the exclusivistic separatism of the Shammaites, based on their rigid interpretations of the law. He did this by casting blame upon the husband who would use those interpretations as a legalistic basis for divorce. Jesus says nothing which requires divorce if the spouse is unfaithful. Note his word to the adulteress: "Do not sin again" (John 8:11).

7. In the antitheses, of which the divorce saying is a part, Jesus attacks the legalistic fulfillment of righteousness. If the church is to turn the saying of Jesus into a legalism against divorce or remarriage, then to be consistent, it should also treat the other antithetical statements with equal severity. In general, the church in the past has been much more flexible and forgiving with one who is angry with his brother, or who fails to always turn the other cheek, or who may lust with the eye, or who does not always love his enemy.

If Jesus does not mean these sayings to be taken legalistically, then the church should present them as a calling to the consciences of all who follow Christ. They become challenges to walk as disciples of Christ in the power of his Spirit. If one fails in one of these points, then the strong should support the weak, with a spirit of meekness (Gal. 6:1-2). Reproof and rebuke are part of the church's discipling process, but are to be given in a spirit of love and to restore.[9] The church today must take warning at this point, since both the Roman Catholic and the Protestant churches have been guilty of some rigid and legalistic applications of the sayings of Jesus on divorce.

Hendriksen makes a neat summation of the passage:

> Jesus discourages divorce, refutes the rabbinical misinterpretations of the law, reaffirms the law's true meaning (cf. Matt. 5:17, 18), censures the guilty party, defends the innocent, and throughout it all upholds the sacredness and inviolability of the marriage bond as ordained by God![10]

In the light of all these factors, one would make a grievous error to assume that Jesus here gives a legalistic teaching. He does not relegate the weak and disadvantaged wife in a patriarchal world to remain unmarried if, despite all Jesus said, her uncaring husband was to put her away. Such was not the spirit of Jesus or the intent of his teaching. One might add that in today's world of increased women's rights, it now sometimes is the husband who needs the compassionate understanding of our Lord and his church.

Matthew 19:3-9

The earlier discussions of Pharisaic-Jewish background and the exegetical study of Matthew 5 give a framework from which to proceed with interpreting Matthew 19:3-12. This passage gives a better view of the Jewish context than either Mark or Luke, both of which had a Gentile audience in view.

The Test Question

Some Pharisees came to him, and to test him they asked, "Is it lawful for a man to divorce his wife for any cause?" (19:3)

Let us examine four units in this verse:

1. *Pharisees.* Jesus had earlier criticized the Pharisees in his Sermon on the Mount for failing to sense the true spirit of the law relative to divorce (5:31-32). In that passage Jesus did not question the divorce bill as much as the right of the husband to put his wife away. In that sense, he challenges the right of the male in the matter of divorce. Both schools of Pharisees would find this objectionable to their understanding of the males' place in society under the law.

The Scripture does not state whether only the Shammaites

came, or the Hillelites, or perhaps both. The question in this verse, "Is it lawful to divorce one's wife for any cause?" could have been asked by the Shammaites to see if Jesus was on their side against the more permissive position of Hillel. But this is unlikely: they opposed him in so many things, and the questioners come to *test* him rather than to recruit him. Yet if they could show that he was against the Hillelite position of divorce for any cause, they could increase his adversaries by driving a wedge between him and Hillel. But why would they want to do that to someone who agreed with them?

On the other hand, the Hillelites themselves could have come to determine if Jesus was as opposed to their position as his earlier discourse suggested, and perhaps to ridicule him if he was (cf. Matt. 22:23-40).

Another possibility is that the two Pharisaic parties joined together to try to ensnare Jesus since they understood him to have prohibited divorce (as Jesus' disciples apparently thought; 19:10). They therefore tested him with the broadest possible question, "Is it lawful for a man to divorce his wife for *any* cause?" If only the Shammaites came, then they would ask this especially to see if he prohibited what they allowed and even required, divorce for adultery. If they could catch him in opposition to Moses as understood by them, then they would accuse him of heresy and being a false teacher.

Both Pharisaic parties might have been represented in bringing the question, but the concerns seem to be more Shammaite in character: (1) It was more of the Shammaites' nature to try to attack Jesus. (2) Jesus' accusations against the Pharisees were tailored more toward the Shammaites than the Hillelites. (3) The Pharisees obviously were defending the right and even duty to divorce by their appeal to Moses. This was not so much a defense of the Hillelite position as of the whole legal system of divorce and the rights of the husband in his own home.

2. *To test, testing.* This is the present participle for the verb meaning *to try, tempt, test.* There are several instances of the testing of Jesus: Mark 12:13-17, where the Pharisees and the Herodians join to "trap him in what he said" on the question of paying taxes to Caesar; Mark 12:18-27, where the Sadducees ques-

tion him on the resurrection and who of the seven husbands would have the wife in the resurrection; and Matthew 16:1-4, where the Pharisees and the Sadducees join in asking him for a sign from heaven "to test Jesus." In John 8:1-11 the Pharisees also test Jesus against the law of Moses by bringing the woman caught in adultery.

Two things are happening in this testing in Matthew 19: Jesus is being tested by the Pharisees on his previous utterance in Matthew 5:32,[1] and in light of the Pharisaic understanding of the law of Moses.[2]

3. *Is it lawful?* The Pharisees use this phrase when the disciples pick grain on the Sabbath in Matthew 12:2, 4: "Your disciples are doing what is not lawful to do on the sabbath." In their interpretation of the law, this meant that it was not permissible to pick grain on the Sabbath, or to pay tribute to Caesar (22:17), or to put blood money into the temple treasury (27:6). On divorce they are asking Jesus, "Is it permissible according to the law to divorce for *any* cause?" They appear to know of Jesus' opinion given in Matthew 5 and feel that Jesus presents a teaching which differs from either Shammaite or Hillelite interpretation of the law. If this were not the case, then they would not have tested him on this issue.

In Matthew 5 Jesus objects to any superficial obedience to the letter of the law not in accord with the spirit of the law. In the case of divorce, one expects, therefore, that Jesus is not going to set forth a more difficult letter of the law, but rather a call to obedience to the law on the basis of love, conscience, and covenant with God.

Those accustomed to thinking in terms of legalistic obedience to the law would tend to wrongly interpret Jesus' answer in legalistic terms. This is the immediate assumption of the disciples, judging by their response in 19:10: "If such is the case of a man with his wife, it is better not to marry." Jesus tones down that legalistic interpretation of his answer in 19:11-12 (see below, chapter 8).

4. *For any cause.* Many interpreters assume that this phrase centers on the interpretation of Hillel, that divorce according to Deuteronomy 24:1 may be for any reason as long as a bill of di-

vorce is given. We have already looked at this view and concluded that the debate concerns the broader question, more likely instigated by the Shammaites: Is divorce possible at all as a right of the husband?

> [Jesus] answered, "Have you not read that the one who made them at the beginning 'made them male and female,' and said, 'For this reason a man shall leave his father and mother and be joined to his wife, and the two shall become one flesh'?" (19:4-5)

Jesus directs the Pharisees to the earliest statement in the books of Moses on God's ideal will for marriage. With mock surprise, he questions that these specialists in the law could possibly have missed such an important basic principle of marriage. From the beginning of creation, male and female were made for each other, to complement and fulfill each other's needs. From Genesis 2:24, Jesus establishes that the complementary relationship in marriage was designed by God to be monogamous and for life.

Jesus uses a form of argument acceptable in Jewish interpretation: "the more original, the weightier" the law.[3] God's intention for marriage outweighs the ordinances of Moses which were in response to the hardness of men's hearts. In simple terms, Jesus is saying, "There is provision for a divorce bill, to protect the disadvantaged wife, but please don't use it as an excuse or justification for divorce."

On this point, R. V. G. Tasker recognizes two unchangeable factors: (1) the divine ideal for the marital relationship remains the same, and (2) the parties in that relationship remain the same frail creatures who often find it impossible to achieve the ideal goals of that relationship. He believes that it is difficult to establish from this passage that Jesus expected his church to become an "anti-divorce society," which would make no provision for the hardness of men's hearts.[4]

Jesus makes an immediate appeal to the principle in the older law and thereby successfully (1) avoids a head-on clash with Moses, (2) draws on authority based on God's intention for marriage, and not on man's sinful actions, and (3) puts down any justification of divorce on legalistic grounds.

What God Has Joined Together

> So they are no longer two, but one flesh. Therefore what God has joined together, let no one [man] separate. (19:6)

The little word *so* indicates that Jesus is drawing a conclusion from his previous argument. He repeats verse 5b and adds emphasis to his conclusion that *man* (*anthropos*) is not to sever this union. In this passage Jesus stresses the role that the male has in divorce, as shown in these verses of Matthew 19:

4. God made them "male and female" (Greek: *arsen kai thēlu*).

5. "For this reason a *man* shall leave . . . and be joined to his wife. . . ." Here and in later verses, Matthew translates Jesus (who was speaking Aramaic) with the Greek word *anthropos* to refer to the male.

6. "Let not *man* put asunder" (RSV).

7. "Why . . . did Moses command *us* to give a certificate of dismissal and to divorce her?"

8. "It was because *you* were so hard-hearted that Moses allowed *you* to divorce *your* wives."

9. "Whoever divorces *his* wife . . . commits adultery."

10. "His disciples said to him, 'If such is the case of a *man* with his wife, it is better [for a *man*] not to marry." The emphasis here is on the man's responsibility in divorce.

In the interplay between Jesus and the Pharisees, we observe that they want to understand what Jesus says a man may or may not do with his wife. The topic of discussion is divorce, but the real heart of the problem is that Jesus has questioned the traditional unlimited authority of the male to put away his wife. The Jewish understanding of the divorce law rested on the inequality of husband and wife. It is unfortunate and unfair that the divorce bill had ceased to be viewed as an instrument designed for the protection of the victimized wife. Instead, it had become a means to justify the husband's right to divorce.

Let us look at each part of verse 6:

1. *They are no longer two, but one flesh.* God created human beings as male and female, with intellects capable of appreciating lasting and loyal relationships and with a complementary sexuality essential for reproduction of children. God designed a one-

flesh union to fulfill these needs. The physical consummation of the marriage act brings about a union that is intended to be unique out of all of their relationships. It is a violation of this uniqueness when a husband or wife goes outside of that marriage for their physical or passionate satisfaction. God also calls some to be single, and they *too* are complete persons, made in God's image (see below, chapters 8-9).

2. *Therefore what God has joined together.* This does not suggest that God makes marriages in heaven, creating John Jones specifically for Mary Smith. It does, however, imply that God unites the husband and wife in marriage, with the mutual satisfaction one of the other in a faithful, monogamous lifelong relationship.

In the age of the early church fathers, the nature of the marriage bond was viewed as a lifetime commitment which *ought* not to be dissolved. In the medieval period, marriage was considered to be a real union which *could* not be dissolved.[5] The modern church has been influenced by the medieval view more than by the patristic, at least until the last decade or two. The doctrine of indissolubility served a high ideal in a legalistic manner, for the church was not willing to recognize marital failure even when it was obvious.

3. *Let not man put asunder* (RSV). The negative imperative in this verb gives a strong sense of direction for the male in the marriage. If Jesus were speaking of the divorce situation in today's world, he would apply it to male and female alike. This imperative does not imply that the marriage is indissoluble, but rather the reverse. The fact that Jesus had to utter such a command presupposes the possibility of choice in maintaining or destroying the marriage. This is in keeping with the reality of the situation, both then and now.

There should be a tenacity even in faulty marriage relationships. Such was illustrated in the reference to Israel as the wife of Yahweh (Hos. 2—3). Israel's unfaithfulness was described as adultery (Hos. 2:2; 3:1, 3; Jer. 9:2-3). In the history of Israel, God punished the people's occasional promiscuity (a metaphor for breaking God's covenant, and also often literally occurring in pagan religious practices). But God did not divorce or break off branches of the Israelites until their persistent unfaithfulness had taken all joy out of the relationship (Hos. 1:8-9; Rom. 11:20). Even then God leaves the door open for those who will come under a new marital covenant based on grace and faith rather than works (Rom. 11).

The Pharisaic Defense

The answer that Jesus gives the Pharisees sounds like a law against divorce to the legalists, so they then turn to Moses' decree in Deuteronomy 24:1 to defend their own position.

> They said to him, "Why then did Moses command us to give a certificate of dismissal and to divorce her?"
> He said to them, "It was because you were so hard-hearted that Moses allowed you to divorce your wives, but from the beginning it was not so." (Matt. 19:7-8)

The Pharisees' question in verse 7 indicates that they understand Moses' statement in Deuteronomy to be part of the law and giving a command which justifies divorce. Jesus sees it only as a permission, an allowance, a concession to them to give the bill of divorce because of the hardness of their hearts in putting away their wives without adequate cause. It was an accommodation to the patriarchal right of the male, providing some regulation to protect the wife from the whim of her husband. What the Pharisees rely on wasn't a command at all: "From the beginning it was not so."

If the followers of Hillel are in the crowd, seeking justification for divorce for *any* cause, then they have no satisfaction. If the Shammaites seek to find some legalistic justification for divorce only for the cause of adultery, then they too are confronted, not with some limited license to divorce, but with the ultimate will of God.[6] But since the Pharisees come to test him, it is likely that what they really hope for is an opinion which differs with Moses by which they can accuse and condemn him. Instead, Jesus places them in the role of defender of their poor interpretations of the law.

Jesus' Declaration on Divorce

And I say to you, whoever divorces his wife, except for unchastity, and marries another commits adultery.[7] (19:9)

If we make a comparison between the record of Matthew and Mark, we find that Mark places this saying in a context where it is not spoken to the Pharisees, but later to his questioning disciples. I have decided to work chiefly from the Matthean account because it more clearly portrays the situation from the Jewish setting of Jesus' ministry (see above, chapter 4).

And I say unto you. This sounds much like the antithetical formula used by Jesus in Matthew 5:22, 28, 32, 34, 39, and 44, but there is a significant difference. He is not here using the emphatic *I* (Greek: *egō*) as in Matthew 5, where he contrasts the true spirit of the law with the traditional, handed-down interpretations. The emphasis here might rather be placed on the *unto you.* Jesus is addressing the Pharisees regarding the guilt of the man who marries following divorce, in a case where the wife is not already guilty of unchastity. He will, himself, be responsible for the adulteration of his first marriage. He *commits adultery.* This is a point not offered in the Matthew 5 discourse.

So now Jesus covers all the bases. It is possible for the irresponsible husband to be guilty of (1) adultery through lust (5:28), (2) making his wife an adulteress by divorcing her (5:32), (3) setting the stage for her second husband to commit adultery (5:32), and/or (4) committing adultery, himself, by marrying another against the divine will for his first marriage (19:9). All of this adds up to an outright attack on the abuse of the patriarchal right of the male to put away his wife for no good cause.

The content of 19:9, without the excepting clause, is carried in the accounts of Mark 10:11 and Luke 16:18a: "Whoever divorces his wife and marries another commits adultery." That which is adulterated is not so much the subsequent marriage union; instead, the former union is adulterated by the second marriage, made possible by the first husband divorcing his wife. Thus the first husband bears responsibility for committing adultery when he marries another (19:9) and for causing his divorced wife to commit adultery (5:32); and the second husband commits adultery in marrying a divorced woman (5:32).

The bill of divorce formed a legal and scriptural[8] basis for re-marriage, but it remained for a second physical union to finally break the first one-flesh union. Until the second union, the first could be resumed without remarriage, according to Jewish law.[9]

Once the second marriage is consummated, it adulterates the first forever. This is the sense of the present tense of the Greek verb *moichatai*, meaning *he/she adulterates*. Even if they were to undo the second marriage, and the husband were to return to his first wife, it would not cancel the adulteration. Rather, according to Deuteronomy 24:4, the second marriage now adulterates the first/third marriage and would be an abomination. The durative sense of the present tense should not be forced to mean that each occasion of sexual union in the second marriage is a perpetual sin of adultery. The first occasion was sufficient to adulterate the divine ideal of marriage.

Jesus is not making a statement contrary to the law. Instead, he elevates the divine intention for marriage as stated in the law in Genesis 1:27 and 2:24. It is obvious from his attack on the legalism of the Pharisees that he was not setting out a stricter legalism. He was upholding marriage without negating the value of the divorce bill where the hardness of men's hearts persists. He was calling for a more responsible application of the assumed patriarchal right of the husband, so that all men would, with good conscience, fulfill God's will in their marriage relationship.

In this last point, the truly shocking thing that he was doing was to state that the divorcing husband would adulterate his first marriage or cause someone else to adulterate it. Jewish men had been accustomed to divorce without such a charge being laid against them. The important question that must be decided is whether he meant this point to be applied in a legalistic way, or whether he was bringing out the spiritual implications of divorce which all men (and women, eventually) must face with good conscience.

The Excepting Clause

Except for unchastity. Much has been written about this clause.[10] We will examine some of the more prominent views:

View 1. Several scholars consider the clause to be an addition to the text, since it appears to be opposing the spirit of the whole context. In opposition to this view, it should be noted that (1) the manuscript evidence favors its inclusion, (2) the practice of divorce for adultery was already an established part of Jewish law, and (3) it does not oppose the spirit of the context (prohibition of divorce) if it is taken to qualify the guilt of the husband when he divorces an unfaithful wife.

View 2. Several Roman Catholic scholars interpret *porneia* (unchastity) as an illegal union and therefore call for an annulment rather than divorce.[11] One takes *porneia* to be an illicit marital union (Lev. 18:6-18), another to mean an incestuous union, and another to be a consanguineous union (marriage to a close relative).

In opposition to this view are two arguments: The frequency of such illegal marriages would hardly have been great enough to call for Jesus to speak of it here as an exception. Further, Fitzmyer's arguments seem to ignore the common debate between Shammai and Hillel. Surely if this was an understood meaning for *porneia* in the time of Christ, it would have been represented by these schools of thought.

Coiner,[12] in his excellent synopsis of the various interpretations of the excepting clause, gives a considerable list of church fathers and their varying views. Several hold that fornication, generally interpreted as adultery, gives the right to the husband to divorce, but say nothing of his right to remarry. Others believed the husband had the right to divorce for adultery and had the right to remarry, and still others were against all remarriage following divorce.

Augustine was among the latter group, but went even further. He did not really believe divorce to be possible and held to the indissolubility of marriage. In cases of *porneia,* he did allow for separation from bed and board. Nothing conclusive can be drawn from the Church Fathers on this, but it is easy to see that Augustine has greatly influenced the Roman Catholic Church and its subsequent interpretations on the subject of divorce.

View 3. Porneia is premarital unchastity which was not discovered until after the marriage (Deut. 22:20-21). Abel Isaksson[13] argues that *porneia* does not as a rule mean adultery. He sees divorce more as a canceling of an unfulfilled "contract of sale."

In opposition to this view, we see that the interpretation does not fit smoothly into Jesus' statement. It would not have been a common application and adds nothing to the point that Jesus is making. If this was the chief or only meaning for *porneia*, then it would have been expressed in the debate between the Shammaites and the Hillelites.

View 4. Porneia is adultery or some indiscretion that could be interpreted as a seriously immoral or immodest act and justifies divorce, and it is the only legal basis for divorce. This is the view of Shammai and his school.[14] Positions 2 and 3 above ignore the Shammaite-Hillelite debate on the meaning of "indecent act" or "uncleanness" (KJV) in Deuteronomy 24:1. When the Pharisees come questioning Jesus, there is no doubt that they want him to clarify his earlier statements in this debate and to say whether he differs with Moses on the right of the husband to divorce.

In response to this interpretation: (1) Jesus is not approving divorce for adultery; he is clarifying what is not adulterous, with respect to the guilt of the male who used or abused his right to divorce. The Pharisees are asking "Can a man divorce his wife for any cause?" Jesus is saying, "No, a man can not divorce his wife for any cause without guilt, unless his wife has already committed adultery."

(2) In this answer, Jesus is not siding with the Shammaites, who limit the reasons for divorce to adultery only, and who believe they have a law that requires the husband to put away an adulterous wife.[15] Their legalistic approach to the law and its oral traditions has irked Jesus.

(3) There is no room in this interpretation for the kind of gracious response to sinners that is typical of Jesus.

(4) The Shammaites were some of Jesus' bitterest enemies. It is hardly likely that he saw theirs to be a truly righteous response to the law.

View 5. The most favorable view is that *porneia* does refer to adultery, but not as the *only* legal basis for divorce, as the Shammaites hold. Rather, *porneia* refers to the guilt of the wife who committed adultery. I offer a paraphrase: "Whoever divorces his wife, unless she is already guilty of having committed adultery, and who marries another commits adultery." In Jesus' attack against the abuse of the patriarchal right to divorce, this one phrase, this exception, limits the guilt of the husband. When the wife is chaste, the husband cannot be justified by invoking his patriarchal right. Jesus is standing against Hillel's position of divorce for any cause.

In support of the above, Dean Fielding states that the excepting phrase means "that if the wife has already committed adultery, her husband cannot be held guilty of driving her into it by divorcing her."[16] Coiner cites the similar viewpoint of Hauck and Schulz in a word study on *porneia:* "The sense of the parenthetical exception, then, is not to give the Christian husband the right to a divorce in the case of unfaithfulness on the part of his wife, but that the husband shall be free of all blame when a legally unavoidable separation takes place because the wife has made the continuation of the marriage impossible through her conduct."[17] Divorce was already required for such conduct under the Jewish law current in Jesus day.[18]

Conclusions and Applications

By this time we have noticed *three themes* which influence one's interpretation of Jesus on divorce. (1) Jesus is not a legalist, and he attacks legalistic piety, especially as interpreted by the Pharisees of the school of Shammai. (2) He is also concerned that, on the basis of past interpretations of the law, husbands have been abusing their patriarchal right. Jesus is ready to sharply confront their self-righteous approach to divorce. (3) A further theme has to do with Jesus' acceptance of common sinners (*'am ha-arets*), his ministry to them, his comfortableness with them, and his willingness to forgive and help them.

For these reasons, the best interpretation of the excepting clause is a nonlegalistic one, limiting the guilt of the husband if his wife has already been unfaithful. It is not a justification of divorce, in the event of a wife's adultery, but rather a call to do the will of God in fulfilling the divine intention for marriage. Neither does Jesus give an outright prohibition of divorce, since it has already been established from rulings in Exodus 21 and

Deuteronomy 21 that God is concerned for the welfare of a wife who is being abused or neglected in a marriage with an uncaring husband. According to these laws, if a man will not do his duty by his wife, then he is to divorce her, so that she might remarry.

If Jesus were simply siding with Shammai on the meaning of the "unseemly thing" in his use of *porneia*, then it would not shock his disciples in such a decided way. This is a view with which they are familiar, even though they may prefer the more lenient position of Hillel. The disciples really thought they heard Jesus saying that there was no cause for divorce whatsoever, no escape from a marriage.

Jesus is making a positive statement that it is God's intention that marriage should be monogamous and for life, and that one may be held guilty of adultery who breaks that ideal. He is not specifically recommending the putting away of an adulterous wife, though he is no doubt aware of the existing Pharisaic law which required it. Neither is Jesus directly saying whether one may marry or not following divorce, though his line of reasoning anticipates that happening.

We turn next to the disciples' response to Jesus and his tempering answer to them. A comparison with Mark 10:10 suggests that 19:10-12 occurs in a private discussion in a house with the disciples.

8

Matthew 19:10-12

His disciples said to him, "If such is the case of a man with his wife, it is better not to marry." (19:10)

It seems obvious that the disciples are taking Jesus' statement in verse 9 in a legalistic way; they thought it would be better not to marry than to marry with no exit except to be guilty of adultery for divorce and remarriage. In Jesus' response to them, we learn that all he said in his answer to the Pharisees cannot be applied legalistically. But disciples must face his teaching with good conscience and apply it in each life according to one's calling and ability.

Better Not to Marry?

If such is the case of a man with his wife. The disciples imply that Jesus is saying that a man in a bad marriage cannot get out of it without being guilty of adultery. If this is so, it would be better not to marry, to remain celibate.

But he said to them, "Not everyone can accept this teaching, but only those to whom it is given. For there are eunuchs who have been so from birth, and there are eunuchs who have been made

eunuchs by others, and there are eunuchs who have made themselves eunuchs for the sake of the kingdom of heaven. Let anyone
accept this who can. (19:11-12)

Not everyone can accept this teaching. It is critical that we determine the meaning of *this teaching* or *saying*. There are three possibilities, of which the third is best.

View 1. It refers to the disciples' saying on celibacy, "It is better
not to marry." This is to be rejected, since in the context the saying was given to Jesus by his disciples. It would mean that Jesus
was the rare one who could accept the statement of the disciples.

View 2. Some Roman Catholic scholars hold that *this saying*
refers to Jesus' teaching on celibacy in 19:11-12.[1] In rejecting this
view, we note that within the context of 19:10-12, Jesus has not
yet made his statement on the eunuchs. This view forces the
sense of the passage and makes only the disciples the recipient
of the saying. This has been a traditional interpretation for Catholic scholars, yet Blinzler and Balducelli have attempted to mod-
ify and retain this view.[2] They think that Jesus sets forth his strin-
gent position on marriage (19:3-9) and doesn't retract it in the
face of the disciples' question. Instead, he illustrates that at least
for some, continence after a broken marriage is possible (19:11-
12), but this is not something everyone can accept. Kodell notes
that Blinzler has received wide support for his position.

View 3. The third and preferable meaning for *this saying* is
close to that of Blinzler. It refers to some or all of Jesus' pro-
nouncement of the will of God for marriage. The offensive part
of Jesus's statement is likely the area that ascribes guilt of adultery to the husband who abuses his patriarchal right in divorcing
his faithful wife. The disciples understand Jesus to say that once
married they should stay married, and if divorced for a non-
adulterous cause, they could be guilty of adultery in remarriage.
How can they receive this?

Could the Pharisees receive this teaching? They come with
their testing question, and to them this rigorous answer is given,
yet Jesus is likely not referring here to the Pharisees. They bait
him with a legal question and look for a legal answer. The answer Jesus gives them is no legalism. It is a call to discipleship

within marriage and in the spirit of true righteousness. That the Pharisees hear his reply as a legalism is their problem. Good enough for them! Let them struggle with it!

The Gift to Be Married

Only those to whom it is given. This should be interpreted in the sense of "only those who have been given ability to cope with the duties of marriage." The Greek word for *accept* means *to grasp, comprehend,* or *yield accordance to.* The verb in the perfect passive (*dedotai*), *has been given,* carries the sense that "not all can grasp or yield accordance to this ideal of marriage, with its responsibilities, but only those to whom power and ability has been given from God."

For there are eunuchs . . . for the sake of the kingdom of heaven. Thus Jesus continues in verse 12. He responds to the disciples' suggestion of celibacy by explaining that some are celibate by birth (from a physical deformity or disability), others through castration, and still others by choice with a sense of dedication or calling, but it is not the sort of thing that one should choose for another. The apostle Paul in 1 Corinthians 7 admits that it would be good for all to be single in the light of urgency of the missionary task, threatening danger, and nearness of the Lord's coming. But each has a particular gift from God, whether to be married or to be single (1 Cor. 7:7-8).

Let anyone accept this who can. The notion of the ability to live on that high plain is brought out even more forcefully in the last sentence of verse 12. We paraphrase: "The one who is able to grasp and practice it, let that one grasp and practice it!" The participle *dunamenos* means *the one who is able* and suggests that there must be the ability in order to fulfill the teaching.

Judaism viewed marriage as normal in life (Isa. 4:1). Celibates could be regarded as socially irresponsible and not helping to "fill the earth" (Gen. 1:28). In contrast, Jesus affirms marriage and also honors celibacy as a way of giving complete devotion to the work of the kingdom. Later church leaders were careful to honor marriage, honor singleness, and to forbid neither (1 Cor. 7; 9:5; Heb. 13:4; 1 Tim. 4:1-5; compulsory celibacy is considered a heresy).

Conclusions and Applications

Does Jesus expect all those who are divorced to remain celibate? Not in any legalistic sense. He knows that the nature of human beings is well fulfilled within marriage. Many have a gift for being faithful in marriage. But some may be able to choose celibacy for the sake of serving the kingdom of heaven. Coiner says Jesus' disciples heard him say clearly, "No divorce!" In response to their shock, Jesus in verse 11 is saying, "Compliance with its unmitigated rigor is a grace granted to some and withheld from others. 'He that is able to receive it, let him receive it.' "[3]

Where there are marriage failures and divorces, this teaching of Jesus in 19:3-12 ought not to be used in any legalistic sense by the church to require enforced celibacy following divorce. The call of Jesus in this passage is to marriage that endures, and grace and ability from God are needed to accomplish that (19:11). When some are single for reasons beyond their choice or because of a specific sense of call and dedication to the kingdom, that should be respected, too (19:12). But Jesus does not ask the church to require celibacy. His sayings on the subject should not be separated from their Jewish context, where he resists legalism and demonstrates grace and forgiveness.

9

Studies from the Letters

Questions from the Corinthian Church

Paul's seventh chapter of First Corinthians is the longest instructive passage on marriage and divorce contained in the New Testament. This is his response to a letter written to him by the Corinthian church about A.D. 53 or 54. In it they asked a number of questions, some of which may be discerned by a repeated introductory phrase, "Now concerning. . . ."[1] As we examine the relevant content, we may speculate as to underlying and related concerns.

In chapter seven, the content suggests several questions:

1. Since Christ is about to return, and since we are spiritual beings, shouldn't we remain celibate within marriage (7:1-3, 5, 9)?

2. Since Christ is about to return and there is an "impending crisis" (7:26), and since we are spiritual beings, is it even advisable for any believer to marry? For each (7:2)? For unmarried divorced persons (7:15)? For widows (7:8-9)? For virgins (7:25)? For the betrothed (7:36-38)?

3. Should Christian husbands and wives divorce for the kingdom's sake so as to be single of mind as spiritual beings devoted to God, waiting for Christ's early return (7:10-11)?

4. If unbelieving spouses wish to divorce their believing spouses, should the believing spouse resist the divorce? If the divorce happens, should or may believers remarry (7:12-16)?

We need to explore three background influences or tendencies at Corinth. An ascetic and heretical tendency to put down natural and God-given desires was developing in that church and elsewhere.[2] This often did not do justice to God's creation of male and female with their complementary sexual, social, and spiritual nature. The Corinthians may have been influenced by the beginnings of Gnostic thought, which taught that matter was evil, including the physical body and procreation.[3] Their worldview might have been colored by Hellenistic dualism. Some of them may have considered themselves so spiritual that the body had little present or eschatological significance.[4] Perhaps a few Corinthians were opting for a creation-despising celibacy.

A second factor that contributed strongly to the ascetic and even celibate tendencies at Corinth was the extreme sense of the imminent return of Christ. Perhaps it was overrealized eschatology,[5] expecting too much too soon. There were some who arrogantly resisted Paul's leadership (4:6, 18) favoring that of Apollos. They questioned Paul's qualifications (4:3). It is possible that they were becoming too "spiritually minded," or otherworldly, puffed up in their own spirituality. Paul counters this, teaching that they still live in the overlap of the ages (1 Cor. 10:11). They need to live out God's love in this present age, with full attention to physical, sexual, and spiritual dimensions, and being on guard against temptation (1 Cor. 10:6-13).

A third background influence was the sinful surroundings of the busy port city of Corinth. To "corinthianize" was to behave as the Corinthians in the most outrageous forms of carnal desire. Aristophanes had coined this word about the Old Corinth, several centuries earlier. Even in the first century, sexual sin was undoubtedly in abundance in this seaport.[6]

These three tendencies help us understand what was behind the questions of the Corinthian questioners: an unnatural asceticism, an eschatological urgency, and a sexually immoral environment.

Against Divorcing to Be More Spiritual

In 1 Corinthians 7 Paul gives strong instruction to the believers in answering their specific questions with some twenty-one imperatives (commands). These may be roughly divided into three categories:

1. Imperatives regarding the physiological needs of men and women. Paul demonstrates a healthy appreciation for the God-given sexual nature of humans and is not ascetic.

2. Imperatives regarding divorce, which must be understood within the Corinthian context. His rule of 7:10-11 is not universal, forbidding all remarriage, but has application only to the special set of circumstances in the question raised by the Corinthians: should zealous married Christians, living as spiritual beings and/or under the tension of the soon-coming of the Lord, divorce so that they might be single-minded in their devotion to Christ (cf. 7:34-35)?

3. There is an eschatological imperative. Those who are married should live as though they were not, if they can (7:29). This means that marriage is part of "the present form of this world [which] is passing away" (7:31), good for now, but superseded in the fulfillment of the kingdom (15:24; Matt. 22:30; Mark 12:25). Marriage is important, but not all-important, as in Jewish society. Paul defends sexual fulfillment within marriage as God-given. Even against his own personal preferences (7:7), he commends marriage, but this is held in tension with the eschatological view, the imminent end of this world. Paul urges believers, according to their gifts and calling, to be devoted in serving the Lord and not be unduly distracted by the forms of this world.

In our exposition of this chapter we will not attempt to treat every phrase or verse, but only those that help us understand passages that bear directly on the topic of divorce and remarriage.

> It is well for a man not to touch a woman. (7:1)

This is a statement from the Corinthians which Paul cannot accept as is. *Well* or *good* in this case is not a moral good as opposed to evil. Instead, there are certain benefits to a single state, which are not true to the married state. Orthodox Jewry would set the married state above the single state. Paul differs with this because of the urgency of the missionary task and the timing in view of Christ's near return. He considers the great commission to be of more urgency than satisfactions in marriage, so for that reason he recommends the setting aside of some good and natural gifts from God, where one is able (7:7, 17, 20, 24, 26, 32-35, 40).

To touch a woman refers to sexual intercourse within marriage. Paul has already made his opinion clear against premarital and extramarital sex in 6:13-20. So the question here is, "Should one marry at all?" Paul responds that it is good if you don't have to, but since sexual immorality is likely, then "each man should have his own wife and each woman her own husband" (7:2). With the use of the imperative here, Paul counteracts any legalistic ascetic pressures to the contrary.

> But because of cases of sexual immorality.... (7:2-6)

Paul recognizes that there is a reciprocal arrangement involved in the complementary nature of the sexes within marriage, based on God's work in creation. This is shown in the following verses:

Verse 2: Each is to have one's own spouse.

Verse 3: Each is to fulfill one's duty to their spouse. Each has an obligation to the other.

Verse 4: Each has equal authority over the other in this.

Verse 5: Each must stop depriving one another in sexual relations! They both have real sexual needs that otherwise could lead them into temptation. These needs are to be met within marriage.

Verse 6: *This I say by way of concession* . . . refers to that which follows *except* in 7:5. Abstinence must be with mutual agreement and for a limited time.

The God-given basic physiological need outranks the eschatological urgencies, though Paul hopes that the latter will temper the former. On this compare 7:6, 17, 25, 28, 35, 36.

> To the married I give this command—not I but the Lord—that the wife should not separate from her husband (but if she does separate, let her remain unmarried or else be reconciled to her husband), and that the husband should not divorce his wife. (7:10-11)

In contrast to Paul's counsel to the unmarried and widows to remain celibate if they can (7:8-9), Paul says to the married, "I give the command; no not I, Christ gives it."[7] *The wife should not separate from her husband.* The verb is the same as that used by Jesus in Matthew 19:6, "Let no one separate," with reference to divorce. The scene at Corinth assumes Roman law, by which a woman could initiate divorce.[8] It is likely that the sayings behind Matthew 5:31-32 and 19:6 are basic to Paul's teaching here.

The cause of the possible marital separation was not an unbelieving spouse, for Paul deals with that in verses 12-16. Neither was the cause adultery, for both Roman and Jewish law required divorce in such cases; in such an event Paul would have counseled directly as he did elsewhere (1 Cor. 5:1, 11; 6:9, 15-18). If the cause was some basic marital disharmony, one would expect Paul to counsel as in Ephesians 5:21-33.

The real cause of Paul's prohibition of divorce and remarriage must be found in the context and hinges on their question in 7:1: "Is it proper for a man to have normal marital relationships with his wife, considering our spiritual aspirations in the light of Christ's soon return?" If they wonder about this, then they no doubt also are considering or even following the more extreme possibility of *divorce for Jesus' sake.* Zealous Christian couples, and particularly the wives (mentioned first in 7:10), are considering an unnatural asceticism that would call them out of marriage and into a celibate life in order to be more spiritual.

In response to this situation, Paul quotes emphatically from the principle of the Lord against divorce (7:10-11): "The wife should not separate from her husband," and "the husband should not divorce his wife!" If the woman insists on divorcing, then she is to remain unmarried, not to marry someone else. If she decides, in time, to remarry, then she should pick up her relationship with her former husband (who hopefully is waiting), for presumably their separation was not because their relationship had failed, but out of spiritual desires or asceticism. Paul also calls on the husband to follow the same advice.

In this context the prohibition of remarriage makes the most sense. If by religious zeal they separate, then by religious zeal let them remain single, or for the sake of the witness of the church to God's will in marriage, be reconciled! If this idea of separation is initiated more by the wife than the husband, then the husband may be hurting and embarrassed. And if initiated by the husband, the wife may be feeling rejected. If such a separated couple considered marrying anyone else, that would open the testimony of the church to ridicule and embarrassment.

We recognize that Paul is dealing here with a special case. Some of the Corinthians felt the urgency of an overrealized eschatology. Paul himself felt and communicated considerable pressure to share the gospel (9:12, 16; 7:32-35). In spite of these dimensions, he showed a great deal of understanding for the God-given physiological needs of humanity. Therefore, this passage need not and should not be treated as a universal law which forbids both divorce and remarriage.

We can see from this passage (1) that God's ideal will for marriage is a monogamous lifelong relationship; (2) that Christians, both married and unmarried, should live unencumbered in the light of Christ's soon return; and (3) that none of God's created orders, such as marriage, should be transgressed while trying to live in the light of that return. But it cannot be exegetically maintained that Paul universally prohibited divorce or remarriage, except in these remarkable Corinthian circumstances.

Let us note the Jewish training which Paul received, educated at the feet of Gamaliel, that great scholar of the school of Hillel (Acts 22:3; Gal. 1:13-14). Paul understood the debate on the lawful grounds of divorce, and that divorce allowed remarriage of those divorced. It is improbable that he adopted a rule on marriage that failed to face the realities of life. He displays an obvious understanding of sexual passion and of marriage as the only legitimate place for such fulfillment. He would not therefore rule out remarriage after divorce, since it provides for the meeting of such needs.

Paul's Counsel on Mixed Marriages

> If any believer [brother] has a wife who is an unbeliever, and she consents to live with him, he should not divorce her. And if any woman has a husband who is an unbeliever, and he consents to live with her, she should not divorce him. . . . (1 Cor. 7:12-16)

Verses 12-13 make clear the command that if an unbelieving spouse is willing to live with a believing spouse, the latter is not to leave the marriage. The believer should be a holy influence in the household and should not take the first step to break up marriage with an unbeliever.

Verse 14 gives the rationale for verses 12-13: The unbelieving spouse is sanctified by the believing spouse. John Calvin suggested, "The godliness of the one does more to 'sanctify' the marriage than the ungodliness of the other to make it unclean."[9]

Verse 15: *But if the unbelieving partner separates, let it be so.* The Greek imperative of the present tense, middle voice, indicates permission is granted for a separation that has an enduring nature. The Christian should not initiate divorce if the unbelieving spouse will stay, but if the other won't stay, then the believing spouse *is not bound* in such cases, for *God has called us to peace* (from 7:15). There is no enslavement to a marriage where one party quits on the relationship, for that in itself is an adulterating of God's intention for the relationship. The perfect passive of the verb *under bondage* or *enslavement* infers that the Christian "is not subject to any constraint because of the pagan's behavior."[10] Conzelmann holds this to mean that the believer is not bound in principle and is free to remarry.[11] Luther commented on this passage, "If he is free and released, he may change his status, just as though his spouse were dead."[12]

Others suggest that this phrase in verse 15 frees the believer from the marriage to an unbeliever, but that it does not specifically teach remarriage.[13] Paul does not elaborate. But if he means to say that the believer should remain unmarried, he could have spelled that out as he does in verse 11 for what is a marriage of two believers. Since he does not so state, we infer that remarriage after divorce in such cases is generally assumed, as after death of a spouse (7:39).

Wife, for all you know, you might save your husband. Husband, for all you know, you might save your wife (7:16). One may take an optimistic or a pessimistic view of the possibilities. The optimist refers to verses 12-14: "You might be able to save your spouse if you abide in the marriage. After all, the unbelieving spouse has the sanctifying witness of the believing spouse to affect his salvation."

The pessimist sees more uncertainty in verses 15-16: "But if the unbelieving partner desires to separate, let it be so; in such a case the brother or sister is not bound. For God has called us to peace. Wife, how do you know whether you will save your husband? Husband, how do you know whether you will save your wife?" (RSV).[14] It has been suggested by Conzelmann that the *but* of verse 15 breaks off the argument of verse 14 and points to the thought of peace as the higher standpoint.[15] That is, peace is more important than evangelism in an unhappy marriage situation: "For how do you know, O wife, *if* you will save your husband?" and vice versa?

This author inclines more toward the pessimistic view, since it fills the last phrase of verse 15 with meaning. There would be little peace or evangelistic opportunity in a home if the believing spouse insisted that the unbelieving spouse remain against his or her wishes. Peace may also apply to physiological and psychological satisfaction in remarriage, since the former marriage has obviously been less than satisfying. This thought ties in well with the notion of calling and giftedness that is picked up in verse 17.

Up to this point in our study of 1 Corinthians 7, Paul has forbidden divorce in a particular case where two believers are married and one or both are considering divorce to be more spiritual (7:10). If they do separate and divorce for that reason, Paul forbids remarriage, except to be reconciled with the spouse. But in verse 15, Paul does not forbid remarriage for the believer whose unbelieving spouse separates. We therefore infer that in such cases he is not promoting remarriage nor forbidding it.

In Whatever Situation, Remain with God

Let each of you lead the life that the Lord has assigned, to which God called you. . . . (1 Cor. 7:17-24)

Here Paul teaches that believers must accept their lot in life, celibate or married, slave or free, circumcised or uncircumcised. They are not to let social status keep them from utilizing every available opportunity to live for Christ in all conditions in life. Believers should not be anxiously trying to change conditions for themselves because obeying God and belonging to the Lord who redeemed them is of the highest importance.

> Now concerning virgins. . . . (7:25-38)

This phrase indicates that Paul is here taking up another of the questions from Corinth. The section has to do with the unmarried and the betrothed. If this is kept in mind, then statements like verse 27 will not be confusing: *Are you bound to a woman? Do not seek to be free.* The Greek word here for woman, *gunaikos*, may be translated *woman, wife, betrothed wife,* or *widow* in various contexts. Under the heading, *concerning virgins,* it should be understood as *betrothed,* as in the following verses:

Verse 27: Are you betrothed? Seek not to be loosed! Are you loosed from betrothal? Seek not betrothal!

Verse 28: But you young man, if you marry, you haven't sinned; and if a virgin maiden marries, she hasn't sinned.

Verses 29-35: Try to live without distraction.

Verses 36-38: If you can keep your betrothal relationship honorable, do so. If you can't, it will not be a sin to marry.

In all of this Paul is giving advice to those who face the eschatological urgency with mixed emotions. It is not a law that he would force upon them. The key phrase that confuses is in verse 27, and that problem is solved if one bears in mind that it is referring here to betrothal and not marriage.[16] Yet in both Roman and Jewish customs of the time, a divorce bill was necessary to release one cleanly from betrothal.

> A wife is bound as long as her husband lives. But if the husband dies, she is free to marry anyone she wishes, only in the Lord. . . . (1 Cor. 7:39-40)

Paul concludes by shifting back to general principles in verses 39-40. He has already answered the question of Christian spouses divorcing under pressure of spiritual desires or shortness of time (7:10-11), and also the question of the betrothed breaking up for the same reason (7:27-29). His general conclusion is that marriage is for life: *A wife is bound as long as her husband lives.* The question of divorce for reasons other than the above special cases is not even under discussion. Thus this passage should not be used to suggest a universal law opposing divorce in other situations.

The exegetical conclusions from 1 Corinthians 7 bearing on the question of divorce are these:

1. Paul recognizes the general principle, that marriage is for life. God-given physiological needs are to be met within marriage, and the meeting of these needs should not be denied within marriage due to asceticism, unnatural spiritual desires, or the imminent end. Christians should not divorce for such a cause, and if they do, they are commanded not to remarry, or to be reconciled in marriage to their original husband.

2. Inner harmony in the home can be greatly disrupted by an unbelieving spouse refusing to cohabit with a believing spouse. When the unbeliever refuses to stay in the marriage, the believing spouse is freed from that marriage. Divorce and remarriage may be anticipated in such cases. If one is gifted with control, then celibacy is a recommended option.

Examining Romans 7:1-4

> Do you not know, brothers and sisters—for I am speaking to those who know the law—that the law is binding on a person only during that person's lifetime? Thus a married woman is bound by the law to her husband as long as he lives; but if her husband dies, she is discharged from the law concerning the husband. Accordingly, she will be called an adulteress if she lives with another man while her husband is alive.... (Rom. 7:1-4)

At times Romans 7:2-3 is used as though it were a statement of a universal rule forbidding divorce and remarriage because of belief in the indissolubility of marriage. Such is not the case. The point that Paul is making in this passage is that the law, "which held us captive" (7:6), is dead through the body of Christ (7:4). This death frees us for remarriage to another, that is, to Christ. If the law were not dead, then the one who has been under covenant to the law is not free for a new covenantal relationship. The law has dominion over a person as long as that one lives (7:1).

To illustrate, Paul says that a woman is bound to her husband as long as he lives, but is loosed when he is dead (7:2). If she is married to another man while he is alive, then she is an adulteress (7:3). Paul is not introducing the matter of divorce into this discussion. If he were, his illustration does not make sense; under the law, a divorcée was not considered an adulteress upon remarriage.

Those who teach an absolute prohibition of divorce appeal to this passage to rule that only death truly concludes marriage. But as Murray states, we ought not to "fall into the mistake of loading his illustration with more significance than reasonably belongs to it in the context."[17] Guy Duty, Martin Luther, C. E. B. Cranfield, and F. F. Bruce all concur that Paul is not saying anything specific in the passage about divorce.

The Pastoral Epistles

In the pastoral epistles one particular phrase (1 Tim. 3:2, 12; Tit. 1:6) among the qualifications for bishops or elders and deacons deserves attention in this discussion on divorce: *husband of one wife* (KJV, REB, RSV), *married only once* (NRSV), *faithful to his one wife* (NEB) or, as Homer Kent translates it, *a one-woman man*.

This qualification has nothing to do with one's membership in the body of believers. It has to do with qualification for leadership within the body. There are a variety of interpretations to this phrase:

View 1. It could imply that a bishop or deacon must be a married man. This is not probable in light of Matthew 19:12 and 1 Corinthians 7:7-8, where celibacy is encouraged and Paul is single (cf. 1 Cor. 9:5).

View 2. Some take it to mean, as the NRSV puts it, *married only once.* A bishop or deacon whose wife has died, or been divorced, does not remarry.[18] In opposition to this view, Scripture nowhere forbids the remarriage of a man after the death of his wife. In fact, Romans 7:3 and 1 Corinthians 7:39 speak clearly to the freedom of remarriage after the death of the spouse. The remarriage of younger widows is encouraged in 1 Timothy 5:14. This was a special encouragement to the women. The men already understood that they had this privilege. Paul in 1 Corinthians 7:12-16 deals with the case of a believer whose unbelieving spouse breaks up the marriage, and he leaves the door open for the believer to remarry after the divorce: "The brother or sister is not bound." The pastoral epistles do not clearly rule out this possibility for leaders.

View 3. The phrase could be a prohibition of polygamy; a leader of the church should not have two wives at the same time (polygyny).[19] In opposition to this interpretation, we note that polygamy was rare among Jews and Gentiles in the first century, although in the pagan setting there might be relationships with concubines or between slaves which did not have the status of marriage under Roman law. Particularly among Christian converts, a special word against polygamy for a leader was hardly necessary.[20] Roman law favored divorce and remarriage over polygamy.

View 4. Kent reasons that the phrase forbids one who has been divorced and remarried, even if before conversion, from holding office.[21] He feels that former spouses from before conversion could still show up and bring reproach upon the church and its example in leadership. To Kent, God had set the marriage standard for all society and not just for the church.

In opposition to this view, we recognize that all of God's moral standards are for all of society. Why should this one be treated any differently? The gospel was to lift and transform. Paul lists a variety of sinners and tells the believers in Corinth that "such were some of you" (1 Cor. 6:9-11, KJV). To have consistent Christian believers transformed from a life of sin was Christianity at its best. It was Paul who spoke of himself as the "chief of sinners" (1 Tim. 1:15).

View 5. The phrase most probably means that the bishop-elder or deacon should be faithful to his own wife. He is to be *a one-woman man* now that he is a new creation in Christ. Whatever his past may have been, as a Christian believer, he is to be blameless. To be exemplary in one's marital affairs is most visibly expressed in a faithful, enduring marriage. Ellisen suggests that

Paul is speaking to the current situation in the life of the Christian, and not to past life history. The redemptive work of Christ in a life-changing experience liberates one for total service to God, and Paul asks only that these qualities be currently exemplified in the lives of the church leaders.[22]

As mentioned in point four above, for one to have had an immoral past is not a mark against the gospel. Instead, it demonstrates that God can change the lives of those who are open to his Spirit. Paul was changed from a murdering zealot (Gal. 1:13), and the Corinthians were changed from immoral lifestyles (1 Cor. 6:9-11). The Ephesian believers earlier were "dead through . . . trespasses and sins in which [they] once lived, following the course of this world . . . following the desires of flesh . . . children of wrath," *but God* brought salvation (Eph. 2:2-10).

The greatest message of the gospel is that God forgives sin, accepts sinners, transforms lives, and makes them useful in his service, even as leaders in his church. Paul asks for a number of qualities for those who would lead the church, because the office warrants a high standard of example. Many Christians could have failed any number of those qualifications prior to conversion. This should not be forced to say that they must be forever debarred from office, or that one particular sin, such as divorce, should be singled out for more severe discipline than any other failing.

One of the biggest questions for the modern-day church coming out of this phrase, *a one-woman man,* is whether a Christian who has gone through divorce *since* conversion can be a bishop/ elder/pastor or deacon. Let us look at practical experience: If some congregations did not use divorced persons to staff boards and Sunday school classes, they would be drastically short of leaders. Church leadership should certainly be of the highest moral standards, but perhaps it is time to look at some notable moral failures within the Bible story. In the light of these, room may be found for some gracious exceptions.

Abraham put away Hagar at Sarah's insistence. Judah, patriarch of the tribe, visited a harlot, not realizing it was his daughter-in-law. Samson, the deliverer of Israel, visited a Philistine harlot. King David was guilty of adultery and murder.

Hosea, the prophet, was ordered by God to marry a harlot as an illustration of God's own patience with unfaithful Israel. If any of today's church leaders were to examine their thought life and fantasy world, there would be many who would fail under Jesus' lofty definition of adultery.

The least that should be taken from this particular qualification is that anyone desiring the office of a bishop/elder/pastor or deacon must have a lifestyle that demonstrates an enduring faithfulness within that Christian's own marriage. Past failures should be far enough in the past that the church has time to develop confidence in the example the individual currently portrays in any marital situation.

Many would be more comfortable with the phrase *one-woman man* referring to one's marital faithfulness in the total period following conversion. This would mean that a leader who succumbed to marital unfaithfulness has no more opportunity to lead in the church, even after moral rehabilitation over a period of time. Would this not limit God's grace and forgiveness?

One dare not be dogmatic on the interpretation of the phrase *one-woman man* in the living context of the pastoral epistles themselves. It seems obvious that there were numbers within the church who had gone through divorce before conversion, and others whose unbelieving spouses initiated divorce. There was no question of their acceptance in the church, only a question of admission to its highest offices even in the more restrictive interpretations. This is evidence which shows that the custom of remarriage following divorce was acceptable to the New Testament church.

10

Practical Applications of Scripture

The Jewish World

From creation God intended marriage to be a monogamous union for life, in which male and female were each designed to fulfill the needs of the other.

The traditional patriarchal authority invested in the male was abused, as reflected by polygamy and divorces in which selfish husbands put away unwanted wives. Divorce certificates were given to wives even prior to Moses as a means of protecting them, in effect, liberating them from being a "chained one" and thus freeing them for remarriage.

The divorce passage of Deuteronomy 24:1-4 doesn't inaugurate a new law on divorce, but merely regulates an existing custom. Both the Shammaites and the Hillelites used this passage as a Mosaic justification of the divorce practice, but debated the meaning of "some unseemly thing" as the cause of divorce.

The bill of divorce protected the rights of the disadvantaged wife, such as the captured wife or the slave wife, so that she might be freed to remarry. This was with divine sanction through Mosaic legislation.

Eventually the divorce certificate and Deuteronomy 24:1-4 became a justification for divorce through mistaken interpretation and the abuse of the patriarchal right. In due time, when stoning ceased to be the penalty for adultery, rabbinic law required a husband to divorce an adulterous wife. This was the law in Jesus' time.

Jesus' Conflict with the Pharisees

Jesus reacted against the Pharisees, and especially the Shammaites, for their ostentatiousness, separatism from the common folk, hypocrisy, extreme legalism, and their failure to discern the real meaning and spirit of the Mosaic law.

His earliest statement about divorce comes out of the antitheses in Matthew 5 and within the context of his criticism of the failure of the Pharisees to understand the law. One must therefore be careful not to assume that Jesus' statements on marriage and divorce take the same position as either school of the Pharisees. What Jesus does give is a nonlegalistic statement of the highest will of God the Father regarding marriage.

Those who think legalistically in the time of Christ, including both Pharisees and disciples, would tend to take Jesus's statements in a legalistic manner. Jesus is observed to soften this in his personal discourse with his disciples in Matthew 19:10-12.

The Matthean Context

Jesus' sayings on divorce are consistent with the context in which Matthew has placed them. There is adequate evidence to support Jesus' contention with the Pharisees. The Shammaites, in particular, would contend with anyone who taught an interpretation of the law which differed from their own. Since Jesus challenged them in Matthew 5 on the right of the male to divorce, it was only natural that they would seek a further confrontation, as reported in Matthew 19:3-9.

When properly understood, Jesus promoted the ideal will of the Father for marriage, but did not negate a realistic approach to divorce. Matthew brings us closest to the Jewish setting of Jesus' ministry. The twentieth-century church needs to read the historical background until it can see, feel, and think like a first-century Jew. Perhaps then it will understand that Jesus is bringing out the true meaning of the law in such a way that it becomes gospel, which would naturally be an offense to the legalists of his day.

Several scholars, from both sides of the debate over the priority of Mark, consider Matthew to represent the best historical sense of the context and spirit of the sayings of Jesus on divorce. Jesus' sayings on divorce are really an attack against the abuse of the patriarchal authority of the husband. The excepting clauses of Matthew 5 and 19 are not agreement with Shammai (which critics find objectionable), but a qualification of the guilt of the husband who would put away his wife.

Matthew 5

The antitheses serve to illuminate the potential meaning of the law and to reveal the shortcomings of a legalistic approach to it. Jesus attacks the abuse of the patriarchal right of the husband to divorce his wife. He points out the guilt for the husband when he puts away his faithful wife. Jesus is not saying no to a divorce bill when it protects the wife, but he is saying no to the selfish putting away of wives.

By making these radical statements, Jesus is calling men to a higher view of marriage and to their responsibilities as loving husbands. His sayings also display the failure of the Pharisaic system of interpretation.

The durative sense of the present tense in *commits adultery* (5:32) does not mean that every sexual act within the second marriage is a sinful act. Rather, it means that the physical union of the second marriage itself has the lasting effect of adulterating the intention of God and the one-flesh vows of the first union.

Matthew 19

The Pharisees sought to ensnare Jesus over his statements in Matthew 5 because they thought that they heard him give an absolute prohibition of divorce. So they ask, "Is it lawful to divorce for any cause. . . ?" In Jesus' answer, he (1) contends that marriage is intended for life, (2) does not negate the value of the divorce bill for the disadvantaged, (3) calls all men to their responsibilities within marriage, and (4) calls for reexamination of the patriarchal right to divorce in the light of the creative will of God for marriage.

In the Matthean context, the excepting clause qualifies the guilt of the husband if his wife has not committed adultery. That clause is not intended to justify divorce, though it may do that.

In Matthew 19:10-12 Jesus explains to the disciples that it has not been *given* to all persons to cope with the responsibilities of marriage. Experience has shown this to be so. This is not a matter of right or wrong, but simply one of the realities of life. Some may be called to celibacy and be able to fulfill it. This has application to divorced persons as well. Jesus explains that his statement is not to be taken legalistically, but that those who are enabled to keep it should do so. No one is to choose celibacy for another. Such a call does not provide for fulfillment of some aspects of the created nature of humanity, and yet the celibate believer is a whole person in God's sight and may be deeply devoted to the kingdom of heaven. It may be inferred that those divorced persons who cannot live singly will have to live thankfully in remarriage under the gracious provision of forgiveness embodied in the gospel. The legalistic Pharisees were left to grapple with his hard sayings.

First Corinthians 7

Paul respects God's good creation and the basic physiological needs of both male and female and does not permit anything or any directive of his to be interpreted as a legalistic curtailment of the meeting of those needs within marriage.

The will of our Lord is that marriages should not dissolve, but that does not stop such from happening. In a mixed marriage, the believer is to exercise a holy influence in the household and not to initiate divorce. Perhaps the spouse will be saved. If a nonbelieving spouse determines to leave a marriage, the believing spouse is not in bondage to try to stay in the marriage. In this case, the call to peace overrides the call to evangelism, and the believer accepts the decision of the unbelieving spouse. The option to remarry is not spelled out here, but is inferred. Both Paul and his audience would have understood the practice of divorce to have allowed for remarriage.

To Christian couples debating about divorce for unnatural ascetic reasons, for an urgent sense of Christ's imminent return, or for devotion to the Lord, Paul's word is a clear "Don't!" And if they do, they are to remain single or be reconciled! Paul's stated opposition to remarriage is limited to this particular set of circumstances and does not have universal application.

Romans 7

Paul uses marriage as an illustration of the influence of the law upon a person while that one is alive. He does not refer to divorce. As an educated Jew, Paul is familiar with the fact that divorce does remove the wife from obligation to the husband and from his influence. This passage, therefore, has no comment to make on divorce, pro or con.

The Pastoral Epistles

There were remarried divorced persons in the churches, and some interpreters think that Paul means to disqualify them from leadership: *husband of one wife*. If so, then such persons were acceptable in the church, but not in the leadership, for reasons of example.

On the other hand, I maintain that the phrase calls for a leader to be *a one-woman man*. That is a better translation. If this view is correct, then it says that any who would qualify as leaders must be faithful in their marital relationship as a Christian. This need not leave out those who are single. And it would not disqualify those who have been divorced and remarried before their conversion, providing that their current marriage is exemplary.

This view might even provide a working basis to deal with a Christian who yielded to temptation, displayed marital unfaithfulness, and repented. With counseling and cooperation, such a person might be morally rehabilitated over a period of time. After people's confidence in the person is restored and the Lord's leading discerned, some leadership role might be assigned, but with close supervision and probably a change of locale. God's grace is "greater than all our sin," and we want to be open to recognize miracles of grace. And the point still stands, that a leader is to show exemplary faithfulness in any marital relationship and in all conduct of life.

The Gospel and Divorce

The Church's Dilemma

Prior to the introduction of the no-fault divorce, the church as a whole dealt with divorce by legislation at their synods and conferences. Then statistics began to indicate increased divorce rates. Churches would pass motions at their annual or biennial conferences to support their traditional standard for marriage and declare the sinful nature of divorce. These votes were intended to stiffen the moral backbones of their constituents and any who happened to read the newspaper accounts of their legislation.

What most of us didn't realize was that the world and, regretfully, the church's membership were not listening. Our nations were becoming more secular and humanistic, forgetting about God. There was less attempt to legislate morality. Individual rights and freedoms were being increasingly emphasized. The moral message of the Bible was being questioned and rejected by many in the fields of entertainment, education, and law.

Individual Christians and those brought into the church through conversion were frequently making decisions to divorce for a variety of personal reasons. The floodgate was open.

The clergy couldn't stop it; all they could do was to respond to it. The big question was how? If the church is openly receptive to the remarriage of divorced persons, whether the "innocent" or "guilty" party, then will it not give the wrong message to its youth? Should the clergy perform such marriages for divorced persons? Can the divorced become deacons or elders, or Sunday school workers, or even sing in the choir? These were and still are big questions on which denominations and individual church boards have difficulty in making decisions.

The church wants to be compassionate and accepting to those who have gone through the agony of divorce. It finds it much easier to do so with those who have gone through marital separation prior to their entrance into the church. When divorce happens in the midst of a congregation with the circumstances that come with it, the church and its people feel that someone should be disciplined. An example should be made, so that all may learn. This sets a tone in the relationship between the church and the divorced member that often is hard to overcome. For those separated after becoming church members, there are often many years of solitude, guilt, and grief.

That is not to say that church members should not be disciplined for immoral behavior, but simply that in today's world, church discipline is often rejected. If informal gossip is expected to punish offenders, that is damaging to both the divorced and the church. Also, if procedures of discipline are not handled carefully and strictly according to the church's constitution in such matters, then the church could be hit with a lawsuit.

Jesus does outline a model for church discipline through several stages of counseling contacts (Matt. 18:15-22), with an effort to bring a member who sins to repentance and forgiveness. If an erring member does not listen to one counselor, the small group, or the whole church, then the only step left is for the whole congregation to recognize that the unrepentant transgressor has chosen not to be a member and is part of the mission field.

Paul in 1 Corinthians 5:11 likewise teaches that believers should not associate with a brother or sister who is "sexually immoral or greedy, or is an idolater, reviler, drunkard, or robber," and "not even eat with such a one." This is an effort to bring the lapsed member to repentance and a new experience of salvation (1 Cor. 5:5). Unfortunately, when this is followed, the church doesn't seem to know when to let up. In 2 Corinthians 2:6-7, Paul tells the church to ease up, that the punishment is sufficient. Now they need to forgive and comfort the former member who has apparently turned back from the path of sinning and is ready to be restored.

The balance of this book is designed to help the church establish better attitudes toward those who have failed. This approach is based on the model of Jesus and a more gracious and non-legalistic understanding of his teaching on divorce. Over the centuries the church has interpreted Jesus' words in a legalistic fashion and often applied them with uncompromising zeal. As shown above, Jesus did not come down on the side of the legalists of his day. Old interpretations must be challenged and new life must be breathed into our response to Jesus' teachings. We want to follow Jesus in a way consistent with the model of his gracious acceptance of those who failed to reach moral perfection.

Jesus, the Model for the Church in Teaching

There must be some consistency between the spirit and attitude of Jesus toward sinners (see chapter 4, above) and the teaching of Jesus against sin. If Jesus was legalistic in his teaching, then one would expect to see that reflected in his attitude toward those who broke the law.

Harold Haas, in his book *Marriage*, says of Jesus' teaching in Matthew 19:7-9 that he centers our thoughts on God's purposes, while resisting the temptation to set forth new laws. Jesus was more concerned about the relationship of human beings to God and to each other.[1]

When Dwight Small examines Jesus' reaction to the woman caught in adultery (John 8:3-5), he notes that Jesus acts redemptively without enacting the penalty of the law. He feels that "what is permissible in the larger context of New Testament ethics must be permissible in the pastoral ministry of the Church."[2]

This larger view of an interpretative principle for the New Testament is needed in the church today. It is based upon the manner in which Jesus so graciously applied the law to those who had so obviously failed under that law. The value of the law was not discarded, but it was mediated by divine grace. Jesus could forgive sinners without elaborate reference to their sin under the law. Repentance was anticipated, sometimes before any spoken evidence. In this same manner the church must apply the gospel of grace—forgiving, accepting, and lifting sinners under the covering of the cross. Thank God that the cross casts a long shadow!

Let us review the conclusions reached in the expository studies in this book in order to keep the point of Jesus' teaching in view (see chapter 10, above). Jesus objected to the legalistic support of the abuse of the patriarchal right of the male to divorce his wife. He upheld marriage as a lifelong, monogamous relationship. His statements against divorce were directed at the hardness of male hearts. He called these men to their moral responsibility in marriage. His statements favor the inviolability of marriage. But they should not be misconstrued to mean that, when men persist through the hardness of their hearts to put away their wives, a divorce bill should not be given to the wives, freeing them for remarriage.

The Possibility of Remarriage

The possibility of remarriage was never ruled out by Jesus. When one considers the implications of Matthew 19:10-12 (see chapter 8, above), the idea of enforced celibacy was ruled out by Jesus. Each must make such a decision based on ability and giftedness. Despite this, for centuries the church has followed the idea of enforced celibacy for those divorced. It is time for the church to have the courage to teach marital fidelity without the threat of perpetual celibacy to strengthen its cause.

Historically, remarriage was the chief reason for the granting of a bill of divorce in Greek, Roman, and Hebrew cultures in Bible times. Its compassionate purpose was legally to free the wife from the union with her husband. It left her unencumbered for remarriage, and in the Jewish setting endowed her with the *ketubah* or dowry, an assigned sum of money.[3] And when civil law also gave the wife the right to enact divorce, the same compassion was needed for the husband being put away.[4]

God respects the sexual needs of his creation. We totally forget the graciousness of God toward sinners if we suppose that God would condemn the divorced person to perpetual celibacy because of marital failure. Such a restriction would be contrary to the normally created sexual drive. Jesus accepts and forgives the woman of Samaria, who was married five times, divorced perhaps as many times, and is now living common law. This indicates the gracious understanding of God toward people caught in sexual irregularities. One may not suggest from this that Christ condones marital breakdown, but that he forgives it and understands the human need for remarriage.

Exegetically, Jesus' reference to adultery following remarriage ought to be understood, not so much as a reason for not remarrying, but as a reason for not divorcing. Jesus was trying to impress upon males their responsibility, which could not be hidden by clinging to a badly abused patriarchal right, supported by a badly interpreted law in Deuteronomy 24:1-4.

The question in the disciples' mind was not whether the wife put away without cause could remarry; that was always understood to be so. The point Jesus raised was that the husband stood guilty of either adulterating his first marriage or causing his wife to do so. It was fear that the husband could be guilty of adultery that led the disciples to suggest not marrying (Matt. 19:9-10). Even here, Jesus was not prepared to enforce celibacy on the irresponsible husband, but to leave it to them to decide their own ability in the matter. Such a position is only possible because Jesus, the Son of God, forgives sin and understands us in all points in which we are tempted (Heb. 4:14-16).

We therefore conclude that remarriage following divorce may carry with it the moral responsibility for its scarring of the former marriage, and that each must decide the matter of remarriage in their own conscience, sensing God's call, and in the light of their own needs and circumstances. It is precisely at this point that the church, through its clergy and counseling services, needs to identify with the parties in their failure or guilt and to seek to lead them into the redemptive grace and forgiveness of the Lord Jesus.

12

The Church's Witness in Marriage

The Meaning of Marriage

For centuries the Christian church has looked upon marriage as one of its institutions which was to be guarded and protected by itself. This has led the church into giving decrees on marriage and having some legalistic involvement in the lives of its people. Historically, however, marriage belongs to the human race and is not the monopoly of any one religion. Yet most of the world's religions have addressed themselves to the responsibilities of marriage and have established their own ceremonies.

The early Christian church developed some customs in marriage from Roman rites. The use of the ring, wreath, veil, and cake all were foreshadowed in Roman practice.[1] The Christian benediction on marriage began about the end of the first century A.D., but wasn't a condition of validity. Roman law considered mutual consent as the basis of a marriage contract.

With the decline of the Roman Empire, the regulation of ordinances such as marriage was taken out of the hands of the secular realm by the authority of the church.[2] The control by the

church led to Roman canon law and the development of ecclesi-
astical courts. From that time until the disruption of the church-
state association in the sixteenth century, the church controlled
marriage. Even after that, the church had its own ways of applying pressure to see that its moral guidance respecting marriage
was observed.

Only in the past few decades have the persuasive powers of
the church upon society diminished. With the great increase in
the numbers of divorces, both within and outside the church, it
is important that the church realistically reassess its role.

For the human race in general, marriage means a one-flesh
union of two into a "newly created unity."[3] It is based on a covenant between the two and embodies erotic and romantic love,
seasoned with the wisdom and the endurance of unselfish love.
Fidelity until death, according to Genesis 2:24, was part of the
original divine intention for marriage. The commitment of love
in marriage ought to rule out any place for infidelity.

One view, represented by Scudder, says a man and woman by
themselves are psychologically and biologically incomplete.
They need each other to complete one another's existence.[4] C. S.
Lewis expresses the same thought: "The inventor of the human
machine was telling us that its two halves, the male and the female, were made to be combined in pairs, not simply on the sexual level, but totally combined."[5] There is much insight in this
way of thinking, and yet we do not forget that each person is
made in the image of God, whether single or married. Each can
be in the will of God, whether married or single. Fulfillment in
marriage is wonderful and does not preclude personal fulfillment in singleness. Otherwise, we would have to say that Jesus,
Paul, and all other single saints were/are incomplete. One recognizes that to live singly requires its own giftedness, even as marriage does.

Marriage is a natural union deriving from the created order,
necessary in human society.[6] Therefore, it is not exclusively a
Christian institution. The sacredness of marriage is seen in fulfilling God's intention in the order of marriage. The couple involved, whether Christian or not, should be aware of the nature
of their commitment to fulfill their spouse in a complementary

relationship for life. When God established the institution of marriage, it was not intended to be broken by unfaithfulness. This was Jesus' point in Matthew 19:3-6.

The church's witness to marriage therefore must embody the following:

1. The sexes may fully complement and fulfill each other within a commitment in marriage.

2. Such a commitment innately and from creation calls for life-long fidelity and trust.

3. Scripture teaches that God has made provision for humanity's sexual fulfillment within marriage.

What God expects of a Christian marriage, he also ideally expects of any marriage. In practicality, however, the church does seek to clarify the commitment in marriage by delineating the covenant vows between the couple and by conducting the ceremony before the church and usually with the witness of the Christian family.

The church will also set before the couple the example of Christ's love (Eph. 5:21-33), the nature of love as a fruit of the Spirit (Gal. 5:22-25; 1 Cor. 13:4-8), and the directives of Christ for marital faithfulness (Matt. 19:3-9). The church will further embrace the couple in Christian fellowship, providing a strong base for a successful marriage and a community network of support. Emphasizing love and faithfulness is not exclusively Christian, however, although we hope to produce them to a higher degree and quality. Love, fidelity, and fellowship in marriage may appear in other religious communities, too.

Perhaps in the end, the only truly exclusive factor in Christian marriage is that the believing partners are indwelt with the Spirit of Christ. They are united in their faith and hope in Jesus as their risen Savior and Lord, and through the Spirit they seek to fulfill Christian ethics respecting life and marriage. So the church has a moral responsibility to teach, guide, and encourage its people respecting marriage, and even to follow church discipline to confront members who persist in adulterous affairs. In the end, however, marriage belongs to the people. They will have to stand before God for their stewardship in this matter of marriage and remarriage.

The church's concern is to assist in the quality of the marriage that is established. Have the parties involved faced their commitment maturely and responsibly? Would premarital counseling facilitate the success of the marriage? The church in good conscience tries to cover these bases. Yet from observation we know that its greatest contribution is in bringing the parties involved into such a relationship with Christ that the fruit of the Spirit flows within the marriage partners. Unless this is true, the rest is just so much window dressing and easily forgotten.

The church is also concerned about its witness if it participates in the remarriage of divorcees. Is it liable to be misunderstood as condoning marital breakdown? The church needs to develop an educational thrust that will help members understand that despite persons' failures in the past, the church, without encouraging divorce, will stand with those people so enmeshed. The church will redemptively assist them into the forgiveness of both God and the church and will assist them in rebuilding their lives and relationships, including the possibility of remarriage.

It would be helpful for the church to have a theology of marriage. Richard Bondi has suggested five different types.[7] I have combined several features from them with my own additions:

> Christian marriage is a natural entity, part of God's order of creation. It involves a covenant between two people, witnessed by the church, for the establishing of a faithful relationship in which each party seeks to fulfill the other spiritually, psychologically, socially, and sexually. That fulfillment is possible for the Christian who lives under the lordship of Jesus Christ and walks in the fullness and fruit of the Spirit.

Applying Christian Ethics to Marriage

Ethics has to do with a code of conduct for morality and the principles or philosophy which undergird that code. The ethical sense or direction of the Christian does not come from this world. The Christian is a new creation (2 Cor. 5:17), risen with Christ (Col. 3:1-3). Helmut Thielicke points out that because of the expected imminent return of the Lord, "The early church's attitude to the world was one of emphatic and one-sided discontinuity."[8] That is, they lived with little long-term attachment to the world because of the shortness of the hour before the end. This is illustrated in the study of 1 Corinthians 7, where believers even thought of divorcing because of spiritual desires or eschatological urgency (see chapter 9, above).

Thielicke feels that this one-sidedness is made impossible for Christians today because of the delay of the *parousia* (the Lord's return). The old age and the new age intersect in the believer. Jesus radicalizes the law in Matthew 5:21-48, imposing its demands upon us as if the new age of the kingdom was already upon us, though we must still live in the world. Ethics has its place "in the field of tension between the old and new aeons."[9] We battle the flesh in the power of the Spirit while anticipating Christ's coming, but we also live anticipating retirement in Florida or Oregon. How we live, and what guides our lifestyle, has to do with Christian ethics.

"The promise of the Gospel precedes the ethical claim in the teaching of Jesus . . . in the sermon on the Mount."[10] That is, the indicative precedes the imperative. The fact of our identification with Christ—dead with him, risen with him, seated with him, and clean through his Word—is in the indicative mood in the Greek. This represents our position through faith in Christ, what has already happened to us. The ethical claims come to us in the imperative, which is not only the mood of command, but embodies in it the potential of new life, much fruit, vibrant marriages, the ability to withstand Satan's attack, and fulfilling God's purposes.

The new obedience for the Christian is not determined by a legalistic fulfilling of the law, but of obeying the Spirit. Scudder puts it this way: "ought" is the language of ideals, while "must" is the language of the law. "It is not the task of the Christian ethicist to set forth a code of laws and demand that they must be obeyed. It is his task to set forth those ethical ideals which men ought obediently to put into practice."[11] The law still exerts an influence, but our motivation is different. Because it is God's will, we have become loving subjects.[12]

The Spirit is the motivator of good fruit (Gal. 5:22-25), which is the indicative; therefore, "live after the spirit," which is the imperative. The flesh is the motivator of bad fruit (Gal. 5:19-21), and in a Christian that can result in marital breakdown and other sins. Therefore, we are to reprove and rebuke with all long-suffering (2 Tim. 4:2). The strong are to support the weak, restoring such a one with meekness (Gal. 6:1-2). The imperative then assists us with the decision in choosing our source of motivation, either the flesh or the Spirit.

If Christians are to succeed in marital faithfulness and fulfillment, then they must do so in the strength of God's indicative, and under the influence of his imperatives. The indicative isn't an automatic production of holy lives. That is, to be risen with Christ doesn't automatically insure that we will seek those things which are above and that we will mortify the deeds of the flesh. Therefore, the imperative is a corrective influence upon our carnal nature which still has expression as we live between the ages.[13] Self-discipline is needed: we watch and pray to resist temptation (Matt. 26:41); we excel in the work of the Lord (1 Cor. 15:58); and we cultivate and rekindle God's gifts within us (1 Tim. 1:6).

To understand this may help the church to appreciate the problem for those Christians who have failed in their marital covenant. The imperatives should be taught as gospel, for our good, and not for our condemnation. They are not legalistic clubs with which the saints are forced into submission.

The conservative church has frequently been so strong on the imperatives that it has become legalistic, especially so regarding marriage. As a result, few Christians will risk admitting that either their marriage or their morals are anything less than ideal. Yet few, if any, could stand before Jesus' statement, "Let him that is without sin, cast the first stone." If this is true, then why are we so harsh and judgmental toward those whose marriages have openly failed?

Preventing Divorce Through Teaching

"An ounce of prevention is worth a pound of cure" is an old proverb that certainly applies to the care of one's marriage. To be successful in preventing divorce, the church needs to begin with a strong teaching program for the congregation, with special emphasis for the children and young people. There are five major areas that need to be covered: building strength of character, building conviction of belief, building a basis for premarital decision making, building for flexibility and resiliency in relationships, and building family and church support for marriage.

1. *Building strength of character.* Strength of character puts backbone into a marriage. Good character makes for honesty, loyalty, and fairness. One's word is their bond, no matter how difficult the circumstances. When character is strong, adversities such as poverty and sickness can work to strengthen the marriage. Unfaithfulness will be out of the question. Temptations will not be entertained. Patience will be exercised, and love will believe the best and endure all things.

The church fellowship is the central resource through which we can share encouragement. Believers are "to provoke one another to love and good deeds" (Heb. 10:23-25). As we gather regularly and maintain active Christian fellowship, we influence each other to develop good character and obedience to God.

Strength of character can be taught by example, both living and historical. From Joseph we learn fidelity and forgiveness; from Moses, patience and godliness; from Daniel, loyalty without compromise; from Jesus, humility and self-sacrifice; and from Paul, perseverance in the face of hardship.

On a personal note, my parents, George and Rosella, celebrated their seventieth wedding anniversary on September 2, 1990. What an example of character and resilience I have seen over the years! Like many others, they have faced times of difficulty and strain, but they held fast, learned to communicate and forgive, and have shown an exemplary love that will be a challenge for their family to match. Due to ill health and increasing blindness, my mother has been in a nursing home for three years. I have watched my ninety-three-year-old father visit my mother every day except when he was ill. I've seen him, even yet, pick up my mother in his '79 New Yorker and take her to church or out to visit one of the family. When urged to go and visit my sister who lives five hours away, he refuses; he knows mother will miss him. He has set an example of love built on strength of character.

Strength of character is taught in the Bible. "Keep alert, stand firm in your faith, be courageous, be strong. Let all that you do

be done in love" (1 Cor. 16:13-14). "My friends, if anyone is de-
tected in a transgression, you who have received the Spirit
should restore such a one in a spirit of gentleness. Take care that
you yourselves are not tempted" (Gal. 6:1). "Be kind to one another, tenderhearted, forgiving one another, as God in Christ
has forgiven you" (Eph. 4:32). Courses of study that teach and
exemplify strength of character at every age level will help to
prepare our children and young people for the hard tests that
come in marital life. We need a revival of songs like

> Dare to be a Daniel, dare to stand alone,
> Dare to have a purpose firm, and dare to make it known.

In this age when selfish, pleasure-seeking philosophies
predominate the thinking of many, backbone to withstand such
currents is sorely needed.

2. *Building conviction.* Strength of character is guided by and
built upon conviction of belief. Martin Luther's "Here I stand!"
was an example of character guided by conviction—conviction
that was held tenaciously due to strength of character.

In all of this it is important to note that the child of God is not
without divine resources and armament in the building of godly
character and strong convictions (Eph. 6:10-18). The work of the
Holy Spirit is central to this development. The fullness and fruit
of the Spirit are at our disposal. This is an area that needs emphasis repeatedly, so that youth and adults alike learn to draw
upon the Word, the Spirit, and the counsel of fellow believers in
order to do the right thing in every crisis in life and marriage. If
children and youth see the fruit of the Spirit (Gal. 5:22-23) in
their parents and learn to live that way themselves, then there is
a greater likelihood that they will use godly patterns in times of
crisis later in life.

Only the Holy Spirit can truly apply the Word in the life of the
hungry believer so that it bears the fruit of righteousness. Paul
exhorted the Ephesians in 5:18, "Be filled with the Spirit." In the
parallel passage in Colossians 3:16, he commands, "Let the word
of Christ dwell in you richly." To be successful, all counseling
ministries need to be based (1) on a strong teaching program

that helps each believer to absorb the Scripture, and (2) on vibrant opportunities for worship, prayer, and fellowship which bring the believer into the life of the Spirit.

An exercise in role-playing can help in the development of personal convictions. To play a role will help both children and young people to identify with those who have family problems. They should be guided into scriptural responses and dependency upon the Holy Spirit. The following are a few role-playing situations where children are encouraged to fit themselves into the emotions and moods of the characters:

• Mother tells her son or daughter that Daddy is moving out of their home to live somewhere else.

• Mother tries to hold the loyalty of her children by destroying their faith in their father.

• The son or daughter feels rejected by the separating parent, perhaps even guilty, since that parent has broken off communication with them.

• The mother has to learn to forgive her husband who has been unfaithful to her. He's sorry and wants to keep the family together.

Such role-playing can bring great emotional enlightenment. If the exercise is guided carefully and feelings are debriefed, godly convictions will be established and fostered.

Biblical studies on God's intention for marriage and Jesus' call for fidelity within marriage should be emphasized at every age level. This needs to be done with sensitivity to the increasing number of children that come into our churches from broken-home situations. A discussion on the harmful effects of divorce to the family could help to establish determined convictions to bolster them at a later time.

Solid expository preaching on relevant Scriptures is essential to the development of biblical conviction regarding marriage. Practical messages on how to maintain happy homes, to increase communication, to develop family altars, to live within a budget—these will all help to guide families and will establish the pastor as an informed friend in time of need.

3. Building for premarital decision making. The church needs to provide guidance in this area. It can assist prospective couples for marriage by providing premarital courses on marriage, communication, parenting, appreciation of marital roles, budgeting, etc. *Before You Marry* by Peterson and Smith is a valuable workbook containing thirteen lessons for engaged couples. Norman Wright has also produced *Premarital Counseling* which outlines a six-step counseling model and suggests valuable resources for premarital counseling.[14]

During the premarriage counseling, the pastor may find it helpful to suggest that the couple develop a pastor-couple covenant for the future. The purpose of this is to establish in their minds that if a problem ever arises that threatens their marriage, the pastor is committed to assisting them through counseling, and they are committed to seeking such counsel. This may seem artificial and something that could easily be ignored, but such an agreement may lend strength to their resolve to seek help in time of need. This will also make explicit the intention to have an ongoing pastor-couple relationship, for periodic checkups or for crises. Often if couples ask for counseling and support early enough, a critical situation can be avoided.

A pastor-couple covenant could be typed or printed up on a special form and be handed on to the couple with their marriage certificate. It could read as follows:

A Pastor-Couple Covenant

As your pastor, I, _____, pledge my support to you and to the happiness and strength of your marriage. If your home is ever threatened in any way, I will do all that I can to assist you, God helping me.

We, _____ and _____, are committed to the happiness and success of our marriage, God helping us. If a problem shall ever arise that endangers our home, we will seek your counsel or that of one who may follow you as our pastor. We will at least meet with you for a one-year checkup and/or maintain relationship with the pastor of our congregation.

Signed: Pastor _____

Signed: Couple _____

Date: _____

The selection of a marriage partner in the will of God should be of top priority. In trying to make this choice, several areas need to be considered: (1) The wisdom of one's parents is a filter through which this decision should pass. (2) The wisdom of the Scriptures is another basic filter to sift out unwise or carnal decisions. Is the intended partner a Christian? Spiritually minded? Carnally motivated?   (3) Is the relationship a mature one? Stable? Good communication? Balanced or one-sided? Sensitive to each other's needs? (4) Is the timing right? Is it being rushed? Is there a good financial base? Are the couple's educational goals within reach? Too often young people hesitate to present their plans for the scrutiny of mature Christian counselors or parents for fear that they might object. Nevertheless, to receive this objective counsel may give them special insight that will help them to make their choice within God's will.[15]

4. *Building for flexibility and resiliency within marriage.* The church should also lead married couples to an increasing appreciation of the importance of flexibility and resiliency within marriage. Successful adjustments lead to successful marriages. It is part of becoming one in the marriage bond. Ed Wheat recommends a prescription for a superb marriage with the little acrostic BEST, which represents Blessing, Edifying, Sharing, and Touching. I recommend this book to assist a couple in making those important adjustments for a satisfying marriage.[16]

5. *Building support from family and church.* Many orders of service for marriages or hymnals give congregational responses and responses for parents and family members of the couple being married. With the use of these, the church community can identify with the couple and pledge interest, prayers, and supports in their behalf.[17] These reminders in the wedding service can advance understanding of the network of church support for a Christian marriage.

Marriage enrichment seminars can be set up on an annual basis in the local church or in a retreat setting. These can be led by the local pastoral team or utilize a specialist in the field. They open up communication and nurture mutual understanding and appreciation. A one- or two-day seminar will provide an ongoing encouragement to healthy marriages, hopefully, before problems become too difficult.

Support groups can be formed around special needs in order to strengthen resolve to make the marriage work. Family support comes from the example of lifelong marriages that act as role models for those under stress. There is also a need for a family not to be too hasty in showing support for divorce of a loved one in order to remove them from a tough situation. Sometimes what a person is going through is not nearly so difficult as what they may experience from the long-term effects of divorce. Support at the time of stress by family members may give the marriage what it needs to succeed.

The church can show its support for marriage and the home by developing a standard for those who minister in its pulpit, Sunday school classes, and on its leadership boards. I am not suggesting that divorced members can never be used in these positions, but that each case needs to be looked at on its own merit. The Scripture lays down standards for ministry (1 Tim. 3:1-13; Tit. 1:5-16). The church needs to observe any individual coming into leadership over a sufficient period of time. Members need to be assured that the potential leader has developed a consistent, godly lifestyle and shows that whatever failings may have occurred in the past, Christ has made a difference. That difference should be the prominent part of their testimony, or the standard for marriage will be weakened.

Preventing Divorce Through Counseling

Despite the church's efforts to encourage growth in marital relationships, the pastor will still face a share of counseling situations with those having difficulties. The pastor's primary goal will be to assist in reconciliation and communication. The pastor should develop a warm pastoral counseling image that will encourage those needing help to seek his counsel.

If both parties will cooperate, then reconciliation is possible. When a couple begins to talk about separation or divorce, they are usually giving it serious thought. It may still be negotiable, which could be why they are talking about it rather than acting it out. The earlier they can enter into counseling, the better the chance of saving the marriage. If a counselor can help them to do something together of a positive nature, the downward spiral may be halted. A counselor can coach a couple to set some long-term goals for their relationship and then to establish short-term objectives, like stairsteps, to achieve a large goal in marriage.

The pastor's agenda at this critical time should include the following: Arrange for a counseling session with both spouses if at all possible. If that is not possible, meet with the cooperative spouse in order to establish some positive goals. Jay Adams recommends that the counselor (1) secure commitment from the counselee to the counseling process; (2) center the counseling upon the Scripture and the person of Christ; (3) determine if the counselee is a Christian, and if not, seek sensitively to present the gospel of God's grace in Christ; (4) assist the counselee(s) into a habit of regular Bible reading and prayer; (5) give hope by evaluating all self-depreciation, examining the Scriptures for the message of hope, accepting genuine repentance as a first step toward change; (6) help them listen to the feelings of each other and aid them in solving some initial problems, no matter how small, to initiate change and reverse trends; (7) focus on solutions to some key problems; (8) assign homework designed to bring early relief growing out of biblical action; (9) enlist help from significant others, even involving key parties in counseling; and (10) determine what the main problems are.[18]

Adams recommends that the counselor not spend all of the time in the first session gathering data, but to endeavor to find the greatest stress point and to assist the couple to action regarding that. Positive action by the couple at this point can raise hope for an improving relationship based on change. The counselor should set up a future agenda (consider the ten points outlined above) with the couple which could be reviewed for progress at each subsequent counseling session.[19]

For another basis of discussion with the troubled couple, the pastor could consider the four practical ground rules for success as presented by Bernard Harnik: (1) the husband and wife must regard marriage as a total life-embracing community, (2) make the marriage grow and mature, (3) tend their marriage with loving care, and (4) complement each other as persons.[20] On occasion the pastoral counselor may refer the couple to obtain other professional help.

Harnik suggests a number of factors that could obstruct dialogue between the husband and wife: fear of revealing too much about oneself, desire to always be right, too lazy to talk, conditioned to be inhibited, urge to criticize, exaggerated inferiority, desire to dominate the other, preaching or moralizing, misunderstanding or deception, pointless chatter, and giving impertinent, ironic, or angry answers.[21] There are many good books available to assist the pastor in counseling.[22]

The pastor's agenda may involve the use of some evaluation tools such as those put out by Family Life Publications, for example, Marriage Expectations Inventories, or Marriage Climate Analysis.[23] Gene Getz has also produced a *Workbook* for use with his book, *The Measure of a Marriage*.[24] This is an excellent tool for marriage enrichment or for analysis of a troubled marriage. The pastor should also arrange for a spiritually mature couple to team with the troubled husband and wife for fellowship, support, and mentoring.

Along with counseling, the couple should be encouraged to do reading of books that will assist them to better understand the dynamics of successful marriage. *Love Life for Every Married Couple* by Ed Wheat is an excellent book to assist a couple to intimacy within marriage that takes in the spiritual and mental side of intimacy as well as the physical. His list of recommended readings is a good basis for further study.[25] He encourages the reading of Anne Kristin Carroll's *From the Brink of Divorce* as giving "wise, sympathetic advice for the individual caught in a problem marriage."[26] Ed Wheat's *Intended for Pleasure* is an excellent study on the physical relationship within marriage and its biblical foundation.[27] Other helpful writers are David and Vera Mace, and Norman Wright.[28] A pastor could utilize a lay committee to review some of the literature and to adapt an enrichment program for their church.

Almost all pastors have experienced the grief, disappointment, and sense of personal failure in watching a couple whom they personally tried to help, make the decision to divorce. Often the decision is made unilaterally, where one spouse becomes impatient or indifferent with the efforts to improve the relationship and decides to quit trying. That spouse may be frustrated by past attempts to save the marriage, or may have entered into a relationship with someone else and really does not want to give that up. It is here that the church's ministry of love will be severely tested. Seldom are two of these cases alike, and seldom can the percentage of blame for the marital breakdown be accurately assessed.

In these circumstances, the church should continue a ministry of counseling and encouragement to the spouse that is open to it. Ed Wheat has a strong chapter on how to save your marriage alone.[29] This could strengthen the resolve of the deserted spouse not to give up on the marriage too quickly. If the causes of the marriage breakdown can be discovered, then it may help in a future restoration, or barring that, in a second marriage.[30] A small support group could be formed around that spouse and the children to sustain them in prayer and with wise counsel. If they are not impatient, they may see the departed spouse return with a change of heart. Special attention needs to be given to the children during this difficult time.[31]

Efforts to minister to both sides of the situation will be helped considerably if the church is not forced into the role of judge. Sometimes the fault is obvious and admitted, and in such cases the role of the church is a little clearer. On occasion, the church's redemptive attitude has been instrumental in turning around an apparently hopeless situation. If the church takes sides in a judgmental way, it often will alienate one of the parties and hinder the reconciliation.

13

The Church's Ministry in Divorce and Remarriage

A Theology for Failure

To speak of a theology for failure may appear extreme, but not if one considers that the incarnation, death, and resurrection of Jesus was all accomplished to care for the sinful failure of humanity. Fortunately, such grace was not limited in its application to only those sins committed before one's salvation. The emphasis upon the change of life and nature embodied in the new birth has at times led to a perfectionist theology, as if only perfection or total sanctification is really acceptable. Most Christians, however, do excuse sins of one type or another. They usually hold a few cardinal sins to be much more worthy of judgmental reaction. Divorce and remarriage are frequently so treated.

Does the church have a theology for those who have failed in their marriages? The answer is not to lessen God's ethical demand for marriage, but rather to accept that where there are sinful actions, God has dealt with them in Christ. As Frank Peters says, God deals with man's sin and disobedience "redemptively, not punitively, provided, of course, that repentance is in evidence."[1] Peters, in his unpublished paper, has succinctly summarized a theology for those who have failed in marriage:

> How can the church deal redemptively with the divorced and remarried in the church unless she has a theology which permits her to do so? The church must not change the absolute nature of God's ideal, but the church must also minister to those who have fallen below that ideal. . . .
>
> We must not counsel the church to be tolerant. Tolerance, like leniency, precludes grace and forgiveness. Tolerance is a way of overlooking the true nature of the failure, as though it were not a serious thing in the eyes of God. But grace and forgiveness are based on a frank acknowledgement of wrong . . . and an appropriation of God's pardon and restoration in Christ.[2]

Peters goes on to say that the church should share in the failure of the marriage as a corporate body. It should take into account its own lack in failing to minister to the needs of the couple in premarital and postmarital counseling and in ministry during the period of separation.

The church can not be blamed for all the separations or divorces. Yet we are sinners all and can identify with the sins of fellow members, as did the prophet of old: "Woe is me! I am lost, for I am a man of unclean lips, and I live among a people of unclean lips" (Isa. 6:5; cf. Dan. 9:4-14). The pastor and congregation will feel guilt in the failure of a marriage, along with the couple involved.

A theology to deal with divorce is a theology to cover failure and to grant forgiveness. It is difficult for the church to assess guilt in marital breakdown. The party guilty of adultery may have been prompted to it by a spouse who failed in one way or another to meet the social or sexual needs of the other. On occasion, a marriage is entered into on false premises which could be grounds for annulment.

Thielicke is concerned that the church not totally set aside the concept of juristic guilt in favor of a mere principle of incompatibility, since to do so would mean that marriage could be manipulated at will. The sense of guilt can be a deterrent which may safeguard the "more innocent" party against flagrant arbitrariness on the part of the other person.[3]

Guilt has its place, but too strong an emphasis on guilt and punishment can lead to hypocrisy, such as when the Pharisees brought the woman caught in adultery (John 8:3-11). The pastor should not be as interested in establishing guilt as in resolving guilt through repentance and the forgiveness embodied in the gospel.

The breakdown of marriage is not an ethically neutral problem. The demand of the law as gospel continually calls for marital fidelity for the good of all involved. Nevertheless, failure to meet that demand is not unpardonable. The wages of sin is death, according to law, but the gift of God is eternal life, according to the gospel of grace. The ideals of the law will always make their demands for constant responsible choices in the face of temptation. Small contends that legal norms once broken cannot be regained, while ideals, through grace, are regainable.[4] On this basis those who have hopelessly lost a spouse through divorce may arise out of that slough of despondency to rebuild their lives, even in remarriage.

There are many reasons given for modern-day divorce. Society does not support the family unit as it once did. The legal system has made divorce much easier. The pursuit of selfish pleasure has ruined many a marriage. Economic pressure in this age of grasping materialism has increased stress within the home. The decay of moral values in the public media reflects a weakness of character within society.

It is not the church's place to justify divorce by undue attention to the reasons, even though it may empathize with one or both parties involved. The church is commissioned to teach the commands of Christ and to preach the gospel. It can seek to facilitate reconciliation. Where that is impossible, it is called to assist those involved in divorce into the forgiveness of Christ within the framework of repentance. In struggling with this tension, the church needs to be reminded that what God allowed under law, as an accommodation to the sinful actions of man, it has no right to deny, under the tender embrace of God's grace.

The legalism Jesus attacked in Matthew 5, in radicalizing six laws, was the kind that put the stress on the letter of the law and heaped on judgment and condemnation. He did not come into the world to condemn the world, but to save it (John 3:17). The demands Jesus made in Matthew 5 didn't just concern adultery or divorce, but from the emphasis given by the church over the centuries, one would think that this was his only point. If the church has been able to be gracious toward those underachieving five points of the law, then has it any right to be inflexible and unforgiving on one that affects so many?[5]

One final question must be answered in the church's theology of divorce. Does divorce conclude the former union? The Greeks, Romans, and Jews all believed that it did, and they permitted subsequent marriages on that basis. The implication of Deuteronomy 24:1-4 indicates that the severance was so complete that if another union followed, the first pair was not to be married to each other again. In Matthew 19:9 Jesus acknowledged the fact of dissolution, and even of remarriage, though he did assess the blame upon the husband who divorces his wife not guilty of unchastity. The Hebrew word for *divorce* is *keritut* and means a *cutting off*. The Greek word *apoluō* (Matt. 19:9) means *to set free, loose, liberate*. Divorce, then, was a dissolution of the marriage legally. It is likely that the union had been broken in practicality, long before it was legally recognized.

The church can accept that divorce is the acknowledgment of a severed relationship, and even more importantly, the couple themselves may have truly concluded the same. If so, then the church is in a position to assist in the restoration of those parties involved in the fellowship of the church, and in suitable time, in the possible development of meaningful responsible remarriage.

A Theology of Remarriage

Remarriage following divorce was anticipated in all of the ancient laws and even in the statements of Jesus in Matthew 5:31-32 and 19:3-12. Remarriage was what Paul expected, except for the special circumstances in 1 Corinthians 7:10, where a Christian couple, or perhaps one zealous wife, was thinking of divorcing due to spiritual desires or the urgency of the endtime. In

1 Timothy 3 and Titus 1, elders and deacons are to be "a one-woman man," to exemplify faithfulness in any marital relationship. This suggests that there were church members from whom the eldership might be chosen who had a history of unfaithfulness to their wife or had been divorced (see section on the pastoral epistles in chapter 9, above). All of this would imply that remarriage was something that the early church accepted as a normal response to divorce. There is no universal law in Scripture against remarriage.

Dwight Small sees divorce as "a tragic example of the broken conditions which occasioned the redemption which Jesus embodies."[6] Remarriage can become a redemptive occasion. It is in this sense that the church and its clergy may identify with those who remarry, not as a condoning of divorce, but as a true display of the outworking of the forgiving, redemptive gospel.

Divorce, with its potential for remarriage, is an accommodation to human sinful action. The foundation for remarriage theologically must be the acknowledgment of failure in the previous marriage, a repentant attitude, a belief in the grace of God, which permits the rebuilding of relationships, and responsible preparation for eventual marriage. The church is a community of believers, themselves forgiven sinners, who can support and identify with those who repent over past marital failures.

Many have tried to defend the institution of marriage by denying any right to the divorced to remarry. John Milton, who had an unhappy marriage, suggested that the extreme literalist needs to sit down and consider, lest thinking to grip fast the gospel, he is found instead with the canon of law in his fist.[7] Legalism here cannot answer the need for remarriage which is derived from the created order. Marriage, according to Scripture, is still the answer to fulfilling the social and sexual needs of man and woman in many cases.

The church should move with boldness and grace into this area of ministry. Long ago church leaders took the ideal of indissolubility of marriage and made it church law. The Roman Catholic Church has been struggling with this imponderable yoke. It continues to deny the reality of divorce or dissolubility. Yet it seeks to relieve the plight of those desiring remarriage with the church's blessing by establishing numerous church tribunals for the purpose of annulling the previous marriage.

Like the rest of modern society, Roman Catholics are experiencing marital breakdown in increasing numbers. In the United States they granted 700 annulments in 1969; 7000 in 1974; 15,000 in 1975; 18,000 in 1976.[8] Common grounds for annulment are lack of intention to have children, improper consent to marriage (perhaps pressured by a pregnancy), the marriage entered out of fear or force, lack of understanding of the obligations within marriage, prior intent to be unfaithful during marriage, lack of intent to enter a permanent marriage, mental illness, alcoholism at the time of marriage, psychological problems regarding such things as homosexuality at the time of marriage, or immaturity.

No one would deny that at least some of these would be legitimate grounds for annulment. The problem arises for many Catholics when they feel that they must accuse their spouse with some of these things after years of relatively happy marriage and childbearing in order to acquire the rights to remarriage through annulment. All of this points out the need of recognizing the dissolution of marriage as a reality of the fallen state of humanity.

Dwight Small maintains that any justification of remarriage must arise from the reality of grace: the renewing grace of God meets persons in their failure and grants another chance. It is not a matter of personal right, but of God's grace in Christ. The creation order lies behind its need; God's grace lies behind its possibility. Since grace lies behind remarriage, it should therefore be approached in penitence, humility, with counseling, and with the support and love of the church.[9]

Pastoral and Congregational Care for the Divorced

Most pastors would like to have a policy for dealing compassionately with divorced members. To do this, they need to talk through their understandings and procedures with their boards, sharing and gathering counsel. When they are satisfied that they have biblical ground to stand on and congregational leadership cooperating, they need to educate their people.

One of the church's most important and sensitive tasks is to help the congregation to be the mediators of God's forgiveness. If God can forgive marital sins, as Jesus demonstrated for us, can the church also bring itself to forgive those who have gone through divorce in its midst? First the church needs to learn that the cross covers marital failures, and that the Christ of the cross actually went out of his way to demonstrate his love and concern for those who sinned. When this has been grasped, then the church may be ready to develop a *service of closure* that recognizes the reality and finality of a divorce when it takes place.

The law of the land recognizes the dissolving of the marriage bond through divorce, as does the Scripture (Deut. 24:4). With a service of closure for the former marriage, the church can provide a theological framework to help both the congregation and those divorced to come to terms with the whole experience of divorce. A simple service of closure could take place in the weekly worship service prior to or following the pastoral message.

The pastor could assure the congregation that its leaders have been counseling, praying, and processing with the divorced member, and that the pastoral leaders commend the divorced person to the care of the church. Then the pastor can invite the divorced husband or wife (so often there is only one who stays in fellowship with the church) to come and share a careful, discrete statement of what the divorce has meant to them, how they've felt about the breakup of their marriage, and to request the prayers and love of the congregation for them and their family members. If they feel that they've failed in their responsibilities toward their marriage, then they could at this time ask the forgiveness of the Lord and any that may have been hurt by this.

Following this, the congregation could read from the bulletin or a pastoral leader could present a thoughtfully prepared response accepting the statement of the divorced person, declaring forgiveness, and pledging support. Then the pastor could invite the elders or deacons to join him in a circle of prayer around the divorced person, with anointing with oil, requesting the healing of past hurts, offering the forgiveness of the Lord and his church, and promising their support and love for the future. A suitable hymn could be sung.

As an alternative, a more formal service could be conducted by the pastor and deacons/elders just prior to or in conjunction with a special communion service. This should take place fairly soon after the divorce decree has become law, provided that at least one of the parties desires to participate in such a service. The church could anticipate this service with understanding and empathy if the pastor has informed the congregation of the forthcoming decree and requested that the congregation pray during the difficult time to uphold those involved.

Each pastor could work out the content for a service of closure to fit the local circumstances. The pastor might consider the following elements:

1. The pastor could introduce the Service of Closure in the following manner: "Dear friends: A week or two ago, I asked you to pray for _____, since the court was finalizing their divorce. This has happened in the past few days. We realize that this represents some very difficult decisions and a great deal of emotional pain to the entire family. We want them to know that we share with them in this pain and desire to offer our love and support. In an effort to assist them and the church body to come to grips with this, we are now going to join with them in a Service of Closure which recognizes the reality of their divorce. Within the context of the church's theology and pastoral ministry, we will stand with them in the rebuilding of their lives.

"Please join me in the singing of "Gentle Shepherd"[10] (or some other suitable hymn). . . ."

2. "I am now going to read a statement that _____ has prepared." An option here would be to have involved individuals read their own statement. The reading of a written statement of remorse from the divorced husband and/or wife could include their feelings of sadness, guilt, repentance, shame, sense of loss, and if applicable, their frustration at their inability to stop the process of divorce.

It could also include a statement of faith in marriage as God intended it to be. If they honestly feel that they contributed to the marriage breakdown in some way, they could acknowledge that they asked God's forgiveness and healing, and similarly ask that the congregation be gracious toward them in forgiving them and encouraging them further in faith. This statement should not be contrived, but be sincere, simple, concise, and in good taste.

It should not contain the history of the marriage breakdown, nor statements of blame toward their spouse. It is a time for the seeking and granting of forgiveness. The pastor should examine the statement before it is read to make sure that it is discrete.

3. The pastor or one of the deacons/elders could then present a response of forgiveness, love, and acceptance, on behalf of the congregation, or have the congregation read a response from the bulletin. Here is suggested wording: "Dear _____, on behalf of the congregation and Board of Deacons/Elders of this church, we want you to know that our hearts have grieved for you and the disappointment and hurts that you and your family have felt through the dissolution of your marriage. We accept your remorse and extend to you the forgiveness and love of this church family, both now, and in the future. We believe in marriage for life, even as you do. We know that you must be greatly disappointed that something that held so much hope at one point in your life has come to such a sad end. We want you to take strength from us in the days ahead."

4. The pastor could then read the following statement: "I would like to explain that this Service of Closure for the former marriage of _____ is intended to help us as a congregation to face realistically what _____ has gone through and to assist us to accept this with forgiveness and love toward anyone who may have sinned in this regard. We are all sinners who regularly need God's forgiveness for our own failings. This does not mean that we have altered our standards for marriage as taught by our Lord in Matthew 19:4-6, "Have you not read that the one who made them at the beginning 'made them male and female,' and said, 'For this reason a man shall leave his father and mother and be joined to his wife, and the two shall become one flesh'? So they are no longer two, but one flesh. Therefore what God has joined together, let no one separate." We are hereby acknowledging that marriage for life is the will of God, that God is grieved when marriage is broken, that all sin is dealt with in the cross of Christ, and that the church must forgive even as Christ forgives. For these reasons we reach out with wholeness of heart to _____ with our love and forgiveness. And _____, we want you to know that our prayers will surround you in the days ahead."

At this point the pastor could gather the deacons/elders and a few close friends in a circle around the individual and lead in a prayer inviting the grace of God to cover both the individual and the congregation as they go on in serving God with diligence, understanding, kindness, and long-suffering.

5. A suitable closing hymn might be sung such as "Burdens Are Lifted at Calvary," "Amazing Grace," "My Faith Looks Up to Thee," or "At the Cross." A benediction could close the service if this all takes place following a morning service. If it precedes a communion service, then the hymn could lead into the communion time as all who were standing move to their seats.

Personal confession for the right reasons will have a purging effect where the individuals recognize their part in the breakdown of their marriage. The use of communion as a focal point and context for forgiveness could be helpful to both the congregation and the parties involved. Personal prayers of confession during counseling or at the church altar will also help. As Jesus forgives, so must the church. Forgiveness from the church will be like a cup of cold water in his name. Our Master Jesus said, "Just as you did it to one of the least of these who are members of my family, you did it to me." Acceptance by the people into the social and spiritual life of the church is extremely important to a couple seeking to rebuild their marital lives.

Remarriage Policy and Practice

The church will struggle with its own guilt in this redemptive process. Edwin Bontrager, in his fine book, *Divorce and the Faithful Church,* says that the church must overcome this guilt:

> If the minister feels guilty about taking a redemptive approach toward a situation because he is not sure of the scriptural principles or the church's stand—how can either of these hope to mediate forgiveness to the couple? Both pastor and congregation can be so bound by a sense of guilt which results in vacillation and confusion that they are not free to minister to the needs crying out from the depths of brokenness.[11]

The church must determine that its ministry, like that of Jesus, is to be redemptive toward those who have failed, regardless of the nature or category of the sin. With this determined, the church can move toward the acceptance of divorced persons, whether single or remarried, into full membership in the church.

Many churches will grant membership, but refuse to allow their clergy to officiate in the remarriage. This is inconsistent. Such churches apparently accept that the divorce did, in fact, dissolve the former marriage, or they couldn't allow church membership. They obviously don't place divorced persons in the category of the whores of Revelation 21:8, who have their part in the lake of fire. The question for them remains—can they work out a redemptive theology that permits the church's identification with those who have failed in marriage, to the point of assisting them in remarriage?

To condemn the divorced member to perpetual celibacy is not in the spirit of Matthew 19:10-12 and would present a real temptation toward promiscuity. The church, therefore, lovingly recognizes the dilemma of those having frustrated sexual and social needs and stands with them at the time of remarriage.

The Reformed Church of America worked out a policy statement in their General Synod in 1975 which may suggest some helpful guidelines for other churches.

> A pastor may with good conscience officiate in the remarriage of divorced persons if in his judgment, and in the judgment of the congregation's board of elders, the persons have met the following requirements: recognition of personal responsibility for the failure of the former marriage, penitence and an effort to overcome limitations and failures, forgiveness of the former partner, fulfillment of obligations involved in the former marriage, and a willingness to make the new marriage a Christian one by dependence upon Christ and participation in his church.[12]

Other guidelines for the church might be taken from suggestions of the United Lutheran Church of America. Their churches are to make their decisions based on the circumstances in each case, taking into account the following considerations: they reaffirm Christian marriage, see divorce and remarriage as a violation of God's order, but recognize that God accepts sinners and deals with them according to need. The possibility of remarriage is seen in passages like Matthew 5:32; 19:9; and 1 Corinthians 7:15. The final basis for decision is loving concern for members in their actual situation. The divorced must recognize responsibility in the breakup of the former marriage, give evidence of repentance, fulfill obligations, give evidence of Christian faith by witness in the church, understand God's purposes in marriage, and make commitment to those responsibilities.[13]

The Illinois Mennonite Conference adopted a Statement on Divorce and Remarriage at its spring business session in 1990.[14] This is a well-thought-out statement supporting marriage, recognizing sin in marital failure, yet encouraging a realistic and balanced ministry to those going through separation, and ending with a statement on remarriage which includes the following points: Jesus affirmed the intended permanence of marriage. Those seeking divorce and remarriage need to consider their inner motives. Leaving one marriage for the purpose of remarriage is legalized adultery. The statement recognizes the removal of marriage bonds when reconciliation is no longer possible; it accepts remarriage in such cases, but advocates the possibility of celibacy on a voluntary basis. It recommends allowing adequate time for emotional and spiritual restoration before remarriage. The conference encourages open confession of past failures, and moving on in the joy of forgiveness in service and ministry as accepted by the church leadership.

What is important in the above policy statements is that the church takes seriously (1) the divine intention for marriage, (2) the need of the parties involved, (3) the redemptive grace of the gospel, (4) the responsible attitudes of those requesting marriage, and (5) the significant importance of the church's own ministry to the couple and the congregation involved.[15] This responsible approach allows the church to minister to divorced members without compromising its standard on marriage or denying the gospel of grace.

Suppose a church refuses to perform a responsible service to a couple desiring remarriage. Without so intending, it may be giving the following witness: (1) Adherence to rules is more important than the needs of sinners. (2) The gospel provides no second chance for those who fail, especially if they failed after becoming Christians. (3) Humanity's sexual nature, as a part of God's created order, must be denied after the failure of divorce because of God's intention of marriage for life, with no church-sanctioned recourse but celibacy. (4) Grace is restricted by law, when it comes to divorce.

On the other hand, when the church ministers *responsibly* with forgiveness and acceptance, it declares the following: (1) Marriage is of God, part of his created order. (2) Marriage can never be legalistically denied to those who need it and will face it responsibly. (3) God's intent is that marriage provide a fulfillment spiritually, mentally, physically, and socially for the male and female involved. (4) Reconciliation and forgiveness are basic concepts and functioning principles for marriage or remarriage. (5) The church's caring ministry does not cease when marriage failure is imminent, but seeks reconciliation, and failing this, offers *gracious* support through the grievous experience of divorce. (6) The church does not deny the possibility of remarriage, but extends a responsible counseling service and ministry to those who are seeking to rebuild their lives.

There needs to be a proper emphasis on confession of past failure along with sincere efforts at reconciliation. This will help the church to be able to understand the hearts of the parties involved and will make it much easier for the clergy and the congregation to be accepting and sincerely forgiving. There are few things more difficult for a congregation to watch than a marital divorce of two people whom they have known and loved. It will take time for the congregation to be able to accept remarriage, to adjust to the idea, and to observe the sincere remorse and healing in the former husband and wife.

The pastor will need to educate his people as to his procedures and theology in the event of either divorce or remarriage. This would save criticism and help the congregation to respond with redemptive joy on the occasion of a responsible remarriage. In some cases, a pastor may incorporate the confession into the marriage ceremony. Dwight Small suggests the following:

> And they have, in my presence, expressed before God a genuine penitence for such elements of their past marital relationships as call for penitence, submitting themselves to God's forgiving and

liberating grace, and have prayed to him for renewal in their dedication to the common life which they now resolve by faith to establish together. They are here taking that step of faith in the recreating power of God and in his care for their mutual good.[16]

The following prayer of confession was offered during the wedding ceremony of a divorced minister:

Prayer of Confession

Even at times of exquisite happiness like this we must be reminded of how often we have failed to be loving; celebrating the creation of a new family, we remember how often we have taken our own families for granted and failed to see possibilities for fulfillment in them. Two people today are pledging themselves to be "all for" each other, and yet our lives are strewn with pledges seriously made and then lightly broken. We have not loved as we should; we have not been with and for our families as we could, and too often we have been untrue to our commitments. May our participation in the creation of this new relationship help us to reexamine and then renew all our relationships through Jesus Christ our Lord. Amen."[17]

Premarital and postmarital counseling are particularly important on the occasion of remarriage.[18] If the pastor had opportunity to journey through the grief process of divorce with the family, then the groundwork will have been laid to assist with the remarriage. The past must be cared for before the future can be faced. Several months and even years of pastoral care may be necessary to help the divorcing family with the problems of self-identity, guilt, loneliness, confusion, grief, anger, facing responsibilities in past failures, and for future planning.

In preparation for remarriage, the pastor should help the divorced person to deal with emotional hangups over the previous marriage. Has forgiveness been fully granted to the spouse, and fully accepted in oneself? Have they truly availed themselves of the grace and forgiveness of God?

Is the motivation for the next marriage pure and healthy? Is it forced for economic or emotional reasons? Have the children of the parties had time to adjust to the divorced home, let alone a new stepparent?

Has the intended couple realistically resolved the questions of alimony, visitation rights for the children, the matter of discipline, and the role of the former spouse's parents as grandparents to the children?[19]

Role expectations within the new marriage should be opened for discussion. Each couple should also be counseled on how to adjust successfully within the local church, given its particular convictions and customs in respect to divorce and remarriage, especially in the area of leadership within the church.

Books on counseling for divorce, the single life, and remarriage are fairly numerous. Not every book will fully represent the position of a particular pastor or church. A biblical basis for counseling may be gained through the study of this book, along with Bontrager's *Divorce and the Faithful Church,* John Martin's *Divorce and Remarriage: A Perspective for Counseling,* and L. Woodson's *Divorce and the Gospel of Grace.*[20]

Books of special help in the counseling content and process include those by David K. Switzer, *The Minister as Crisis Counselor;* Norman Wright, *An Answer to Divorce;* Bob W. Brown, *Getting Married Again: A Guide for Successful Remarriage;* Jim Smoke, *Growing Through Divorce;* Arnold W. D. Baird and E. Vaughn, *Divorce, Prevention or Survival;* and Gary Collins, *It's Okay to Be Single Again.*[21]

There are many books of testimony of how people have come through divorce to successful single or remarried life. One or two of these in the hands of those involved will help them to face the future with hope.[22]

Some denominations allow their pastors to perform the marriage ceremony for divorced persons, based on their own judgment of the circumstances and attitudes involved. Still others have rigid guidelines by which they must abide.[23] If pastors are forbidden by their denomination to perform marriages for divorced members, they may still offer the following advice to those contemplating remarriage:

1. Seek your pastor's counsel in preparation for marriage. He will help you avoid previous mistakes, consider readiness for marriage in relationship to your former marriage, and offer friendship and ministry to you in your new home.

2. Try to understand why the denomination forbids the pastor to officiate. It probably feels that to do so would compromise the church's witness on the sanctity and enduring nature of marriage. You may disagree with this position, but try to respect both the church and its policies.

3. Some pastors disagree with this stand against remarriage, but until changes are made in their policy statements, they must act in cooperation with their guidelines.

4. The pastor may advise you to have a justice of the peace or a neighboring pastor to officiate. On occasion, they will open their sanctuary for the ceremony, with the outside pastor officiating. They may also open their fellowship hall for the reception, so that the couple doesn't feel estranged from the church's fellowship.

5. Seldom is a church, by its rigid stand, trying to be punitive toward divorced members. Most want to be redemptive without negating their standards on marriage.

6. Pastors may announce the marriage in the church bulletin and welcome the couple publicly. The pastor and the new couple should plan for sessions of postmarital counseling.

14

The Church's Educational Objectives in These Areas

Accepting Jesus as the Role Model

Jesus said that whoever will teach the commandments will be great in the kingdom (Matt. 5:19).

The church may not compromise its commission to teach, but it must temper its attitudes in teaching by careful observance of the model of Jesus, both in his teaching and his acceptance of sinners.

The twofold goal for the church is (1) to teach what Jesus taught, and (2) teach in the manner in which Jesus taught and exemplified it. It must make a serious exegetical study of the relevant Scriptures, using inductive methods and taking into account the historical setting of the author and audience. The church must examine its own dogmatic policies as objectively as possible in order to ascertain any doctrinal or attitudinal deficiencies in the light of Jesus' example.

Marriages Will Fail

The church should uphold the divine intention for marriage. At the same time the church should adopt and make effective a biblical basis for total forgiveness and acceptance of those who, for various reasons, have failed. While the church will do all in its power to save a marriage, it will also accept the fact that some marriages do fail. Thus it must relate as a body to a hurting member with love, forgiveness, and understanding. This should be especially true when, as in the case of the disadvantaged wife of the Old Testament, a husband puts his wife away without good cause, or deserts her.

The Church's Role Under Grace

The church will have to educate its people to see its role, not only as a defender of the faith, but as that of the redemptive, saving arm of Christ to sinners in a fallen world. It is to help those who fall, in the spirit of meekness. If a church in its teaching has emphasized a legalistic approach to imperatives of the Gospels or epistles, it will be difficult for its people to be gracious and forgiving to those who have sinned against those commands.

Churches should courageously help their people to see the gospel and not legalism. To avoid hypocrisy at this point is vital. Honest introspection and admission of personal faults will help the congregation to see that if their sins have been forgiven, then so may those who have been involved in marital failure. Church leaders need to make efforts to alter previous convictions and attitudes until they conform to those of Christ.

Sensitizing the Church

The church would also do well to discreetly expose itself to the feelings and emotions of those who have endured the agony of divorce. Seldom are people so harsh in judgment when once exposed to the hurt, guilt, grief, and loneliness of the divorced and their families.[1]

Divorce has been described by Joseph Epstein as "an emotional ravaging . . . a very private hell."[2] "Whatever else divorce might be . . . it is an enormous personal failure."[3] Lars Granberg has said that "a good many divorced persons have been deeply wronged. Given a choice, many of them would have preferred not to be divorced."[4] Suicide among divorced men and women, according to Granberg, is three to four times higher than among married men and women.[5]

All too often, the church has, by its attitudes regarding marital failure, perpetrated a hardness and indifference toward those involved. In part, this is due to a fear, that to befriend a divorced person is to condone divorce. Yet we freely forgive other sins, even murder, gossip, tax evasion, and the like. It is time for the church to carefully weigh out its attitudes toward marital failure and the ensuing need for remarriage.

The Reeducation Process

To reeducate its people, the church must first study the created nature of the sexes. Then it will come to the realization that neither divorce nor ecclesiastically enforced celibacy can stop the sociological and physiological drives that are innate in man and woman. The church can call its members to celibacy under certain circumstances, but it has no scriptural right to legislate enforced celibacy when God has provided marriage as a legitimate solution to humanity's created urges.[6]

The church should also educate its people to expect their pastoral team to minister redemptively to divorced members, leading to forgiveness from guilt, healing of inner hurts, and restoration and reconciliation in the body of Christ. This ministry will involve counseling prior, during, and following divorce.

Such educational goals may be accomplished through sermons, teaching seminars, and perhaps most effectively through role-playing. This latter assists in assessing old values and establishing new ones.[7]

One method that has worked well in our seminars on divorce is to play musical roles. The group sits in a circle. The various roles are written on cards. One card at a time circulates around the group to music. When the music stops, that person tries to play the role, realizing that others may jump into that role to relieve them or to add to the role. The group relaxes, and those who want to share feel at liberty to be involved. Care needs to be taken not to force people into a role that is too close to their own hurting experience. Some roles that may be represented:

- A divorced person who is facing severe temptation in trying to remain celibate.
- One who yearns to have the companionship of a helpmate to assist in the rearing of a young family.
- One who requests that the pastor perform the ceremony for his proposed remarriage.
- A remarried divorced person who wishes to teach Sunday school, or perhaps to become a deacon.
- Others could play accompanying roles to the above by taking the part of a judgmental and rigid member, of the pastor, deacon, Sunday school teacher, or a member of the church board which must consider the positive and negative aspects of the above requests.

After the role-play, debrief feelings and learnings. You will also want to bring scriptural guidelines into focus in order to guide decision making and the formation of attitudes and values. Group discussion and prayer are valuable in this reeducation process.

Preventive Programs for the Church

The church should develop programs to prevent marriage breakdown and to strengthen the family. Plans should be worked out for sex education programs to complement those given in the homes or the secular setting. Premarital counseling programs and marriage enrichment courses should be established (see the section on counseling in chapter 12, above).

One area in which the church could spend more energy is that of the home as the chief educator in moral values related to sex and marriage. Materials need to be developed or adapted for use in family devotions so that from an early age, communication and education from the parent to the child takes place. If the parents do not establish themselves as the chief sex educators of their children in their early years, then children will take their values from their peers, the humanistic and hedonistic television fare, and their public school health education courses, which are often amoral or relative in their values.

Ministry to singles in the church is developing at a fairly rapid pace. This is one of the fastest growing social groups in many city churches, and the church that ignores the special identity and needs of this group will miss valuable opportunities for both ministry and the development of this group for ministry. Reed and Woodson, among others, offer helpful guidance in developing singles programs.[8]

The survey of the church's ministry in this chapter will need to be adapted to each local church or denomination. It can serve as a basis for discussion and clarification of church policies. Pastoral workshops will be essential to freeing the minister and the church from former unscriptural attitudes and fears. Such programs allow for orientation to fresh exegetical studies and discussion of possible policy changes. Sometimes pastoral leadership may ask a visiting speaker to help the congregation break through to a new expression of God's grace and forgiveness in the area of divorce and remarriage. This should allow for more openness in facing issues first, before application to particular persons and situations.

Concluding Statement

As you have read through this book, we hope several things have happened. You now have a sense of the Jewish setting with its roots in a strong and at times abusive patriarchal society. You sense the legalism which Jesus opposed in his confrontations with the Pharisees. You sense the divine concern for the disadvantaged under any legal system. You sense the tender relationship of Jesus to the common sinner, and his gracious forgiveness so freely given.

As all of this is carried into the interpretation of Jesus' statements on divorce, you grow in realizing that Jesus did not arrive at the legal position of either group of Pharisees, nor did he intend to issue legalistic statements. He did set before all a high standard of marriage without compromise. Yet he was also forgiving and accepting of sinners who failed to live up to that high standard. He did not dispute against the right to remarriage following divorce, but he did contradict the rights of the male to divorce for any cause.

The church has been challenged to follow in the steps of Jesus, to teach as he taught, to love as he loved, to forgive and heal as he forgave and healed. Part of this gospel vision is to walk in the tension of ministry, where the will of God must be declared for marriage, but where grace may abound for the failing. To know when and how to discipline, and when to administer comfort and hope—that will always test the church's understanding of law and grace.

Some in the church have held tenaciously to the highest standards for marriage and have not known how to help the failing. Still others have sensed the hurts and disappointments of the divorced and have yearned to minister to them, but without knowing the biblical basis for such ministry. I hope this interpretative study will help many to find that middle ground where standards rest firmly on the Scripture, and from which a ministry of grace may flow without guilt, as one follows in the steps of the Lord Jesus Christ.

Leader's Guide

This Leader's Guide divides the text into thirteen sessions in order to accommodate a quarterly elective, for use in an adult department of the Sunday school or in a Bible study group.

The Teacher's Preparation

To prepare to teach this text, first survey the book, reading all conclusions or summary statements at the ends of chapters, and especially chapter 10. You will then be able to see where the author is taking you.

Begin with an attitude of openness to truth that you may not have discovered before, and then impart an enthusiasm for this to your students. Establish for yourself that this book supports the highest ideal for marriage as Jesus taught, but that it doesn't see Jesus denying the reality of divorce, or the need for a biblical basis for the church's ministry to divorced persons. I hope that with growing excitement you will discover what the main reasons are for this position.

Be much in prayer over this course. It is so easy to be misunderstood on a subject as sensitive as divorce. We join with God in hating divorce (Mal. 2:16), especially selfish divorce. We agree with God in seeing reason for the compassionate use of divorce to protect the rights of the victim of senseless cruelty (Exod. 21:7-11). We join with Jesus in Matthew 5 and 19 in recognizing the guilt of the male who uses his patriarchal power to put away his wife for no good reason. We also agree with Jesus in Matthew 19:10-12 in not forcing celibacy upon those who have gone through divorce.

One word of caution: some in the class will want to deal with cases. That is, they will know someone who is a candidate for divorce or who has gone through divorce, and they will want you to make a judgment on that situation. This will just embroil you in a fruitless waste of time. Let the class know from the outset that you will not permit this to happen. You will stick to the biblical study until it is finished, and until that time the class is not equipped to handle any case studies. Your goal is to have a biblically educated and merciful church to support duly assigned congregational leaders who deal with specific cases.

The basic approach will be to endorse and nurture marriage for life, and to take a compassionate interest in the needs of divorced persons after the model of Jesus. With the assistance of this book, the class will search for the biblical basis that will free you as a people to have renewed attitudes. Your forgiveness, love, and acceptance will permit those who have fallen to get up and rebuild their lives with the spiritual support of the church.

Since the Leader's Guide is part of this book, we have tried to be brief. There will be more content in the book for each session than you will have time for, so use a highlighter and be selective. My prayers are with you in this glorious teaching task.

Procedure

This Leader's Guide will assume a question-answer and discussion method. It is therefore important for students to have access to the text each week so they can read the assigned section in advance. They should be directed to the questions in this Leader's Guide, so that they may do their reading with the questions in view. Both the teacher and students can be prepared to highlight or underline material pertinent to their answers to the questions. They could earmark each point in the margin; for example for question one, there may be six points that apply to the answer. In the margin, next to the underlined point they would jot in 1.a, 1.b, and so on. In this way they will be able to speak to the question with the material in focus. The lecture method may be the quickest way to cover ground, but the question-discussion method will lead to more active participation and an interesting class. Following are study questions:

Session 1, on the Preface and Chapter 1:
Jewish Marriage Customs and Patriarchy

1. From the Preface: What is the author's ultimate goal? What stages of the learning journey lead to that goal?

2. What problems did polygamy raise for Old Testament marriages?

3. Of what advantage was the dowry to the wife in a marriage, when in fact, it was given by her father to her husband?

4. How does the betrothal arrangement demonstrate the control of the male over the female?

5. How were women abused in the patriarchal society of the Old Testament? Does Genesis 3:16 identify patriarchal abuse or patriarchy itself as part of the fallen human condition? Are we living in a patriarchal society today? What would it take to make patriarchy positive and work well? Review the Scripture references and discuss whether the Bible points beyond patriarchy to a pattern of mutuality and interdependence, or whether patriarchy in Scripture provides room for mutuality and interdependence.

Session 2, on Chapter 2: Jewish Law on Divorce

1. Where did the Jewish law of divorce find its origin? When did Jews abolish the absolute right of the male to divorce his wife at will?

2. In what sense does Deuteronomy 24:1-4 regulate the practice of divorce?

3. How did the interpretation of "something shameful/objectionable/unseemly" (Deut. 24:1) affect the followers of Hillel in their attitude toward divorce?

4. How did God show concern for the slave wife, and for the

captive wife, if the husband was unhappy with them? How is this concern reflected in attitudes of the church today? Is there a parallel between these situations and current spousal abuse?

5. In the Old Testament, how was the practice of allowing divorce demonstrated by certain restrictions on divorce?

6. In the time of Jesus, there was a ruling requiring divorce of the wife if she committed adultery. How might this affect the interpretation of the excepting clause in Matthew 19:9?

7. How do you feel about Hillelite rabbis as "practical people," who didn't try to prevent divorce for cause or by mutual consent? Is the church coming closer to that position today?

8. In the light of certain rabbis' efforts to check divorce, what might the church do that would help to prevent the breakdown of marriage?

9. Under each conclusion is a thought-provoking question intended to help us begin to think about implications for the interpretation of Jesus' sayings on divorce. Discuss one or two of these (number 2, 3, 4, 6, or 7).

Session 3, on Chapter 3: The Pharisees and Jesus

1. How does Jesus' criticism of the Pharisees contrast with their criticism of him? Were both accurate?

2. There were two schools of Pharisees in the time of Jesus, led by Shammai and Hillel. In what ways did they differ?

3. Why did the common people (the *'am ha-arets*) in Jesus' time despise the Pharisees under Shammai?

4. Examine the "woes" of Matthew 23:2-35 with your group. Why do the Shammaites suit these criticisms by Jesus more than the Hillelites?

5. The Shammaites contended that the "unseemly thing" of Deuteronomy 24:1 referred to adultery and that a man could therefore only divorce his wife for adultery. When you consider Jesus' bitter attack on the Shammaites, do you think it likely that Jesus agreed with their legalistic approach to divorce for adultery only? At first glance, that seems to be what Matthew 19:9 is suggesting in the "except for unchastity"clause.

Session 4, on Chapter 4:
Jesus, the Model of Caring for Sinners

1. Examine the Scriptures in the endnote about Jesus being a friend of sinners. Why was this such an aggravation to the Pharisees?

2. Take time to thoroughly examine the case studies of Jesus' friendship to sinners. What attitude or spirit do you find in Jesus that should be carried into the meaning of Jesus' answer to the Pharisees in Matthew 19:9?

3. Observe Jesus' attitude toward the breaking of the strict observance of the Sabbath laws. How can this help us understand the importance of the institution of marriage even to those who may have failed in their own marriages?

4. Three Gospel accounts give us a record of Jesus' sayings on divorce. Why is Matthew's account chosen as the best record for discerning Jesus' meaning?

Session 5, on Chapters 5-6: Matthew 5

1. In what ways did the Pharisees fail to keep the law to Jesus' satisfaction?

2. What was Hillel's basic understanding of Scripture and tradition respecting divorce?

3. Why is it inconsistent to think that Jesus would hold Shammai's point of view on divorce?

4. Matthew 5:27-30: Jesus makes a radical statement about a man who "looks at a woman with lust." (1) On this, explain what Jesus expects of us. Are we really to tear out our eye or cut off our hand? Might this refer to all occasions for lust and the need for self-restraint? (2) If lustful looking adulterates marriage, what about physical abuse, mental cruelty, the workaholic who has no time for family, etc.? (3) Is Jesus speaking legalistically, or emphasizing the covenantal high calling of marriage, difficult as that may be?

5. Matthew 5:31-32: Jesus takes exception to the notion that there is a law in Deuteronomy 24:1-4 which justifies divorce. In doing so, how does he attack the abuse of the patriarchal custom of the husband having authority over his wife?

6. Matthew 5:32: What is the meaning of "commits adultery"

in this context? Does a second marriage perpetuate continuous adulterous acts each time the couple enters the marriage bed? If divorce, as commonly recognized, actually ended all rights of the husband to his former wife, then in what sense does the second husband commit adultery? In what sense is there a breaking of covenant with God and spouse? Consider Matthew 5:28. How far-reaching is the failure of the husband who puts away his wife without cause? Discuss.

7. If Jesus really wasn't speaking legalistically, then how is the church to apply his teachings to the church body today?

Session 6, on Chapter 7: Matthew 19:3-8

1. Matthew 19:3: Why does Ewald think that it was probably the Shammaites who came testing Jesus?

2. Matthew 19:3: What is the significance of the question "Is it lawful?" from the Pharisees' point of view?

3. Matthew 19:4-5: What can we learn from these verses about the intention of God for marriage?

4. Matthew 19:4-5: What points does Jesus score by going back to Genesis 2:24 for his response to the Pharisees?

5. Matthew 19:6: Examine how Jesus implies that the man takes initiative in marriage and divorce in verses 5-9. Who or what is Jesus confronting in this discussion on divorce?

6. Matthew 19:6: Does Jesus imply that it is impossible for the marriage ever to be dissolved, even in the event of a divorce? Or is he teaching that because of the nature of the bond, it should never be violated?

7. Matthew 19:7-8: How does Jesus treat the Pharisees' dependency upon Moses (Deut. 24:1-4) for the justification of the husband's right to divorce his wife?

Session 7, on Chapters 7-8: Matthew 19:9-12

1. What bases does Jesus cover in his attack on the abuse of the patriarchal right of the husband to divorce his wife? (Review Matt. 19:4-9.)

2. In what sense are we to understand "commits adultery" in terms of its impact upon either the first or second marriage? In terms of the placement of guilt? In terms of duration?

3. Why should we reject the Roman Catholic view that the word "unchastity" (Greek: *porneia*) refers to an illegal union?

4. Why is it unlikely that *porneia* means premarital unchastity in this context?

5. Why should we reject Shammai's view, that *porneia*/adultery is the only legal grounds for divorce?

6. Why is a nonlegalistic view of the meaning of "except for unchastity" preferable? In what sense is this more true of Jesus as we know him? How do Ewald's three themes apply here?

7. Matthew 19:10: Why do the disciples think that it would be better not to marry?

8. Matthew 19:11: What is implied in Jesus' words, "Not everyone can accept this teaching, but only those to whom it is given"? And implied in 19:12, "Let anyone accept this who can"? Is Jesus prepared to be gracious toward those who can't? Is Jesus talking about being celibate and single before marriage? after divorce?

Session 8, on Chapter 9: About 1 Corinthians 7

1. To understand Paul's chapter, we need to discern questions the Corinthians want answered. What are they? Study the verses cited, read between the lines, and this chapter becomes exciting.

2. How did these three factors affect the Corinthian church: the ascetic tendency (denial of normal sensual fulfillments), the tendency toward celibacy due to unbalanced spiritual desires and/or the expected early return of Jesus, and the sinful environment?

3. In 7:2-6: How does Paul argue in favor of the satisfaction of one's sexual needs within marriage? How does this respect God's good creation, people as sexual and spiritual beings?

4. In 7:10-11: What is the real cause of Paul's prohibition of divorce and remarriage? Is it because of his opposition to an asceticism which fueled unbalanced spiritual desires—perhaps growing out of expecting the imminent return of Christ?

5. In 7:15: What is the implication of the present imperative command, "Let it be so!"? Does the phrase, "not bound" suggest that remarriage is therefore a possibility?

6. What conclusions can be drawn from Paul's teaching in this

chapter that specifically relate to marriage and divorce?

Session 9, on Chapters 9-10:
Romans, the Pastorals, and Applications

1. What is the argument against Romans 7:1-4 being used to condemn divorce and remarriage as long as a former spouse is living?

2. What is the problem with interpreting "husband of one wife" in 1 Timothy 3:2 and 12 as "married only once"? Or as a prohibition of polygamy? Who is "a one-woman man"?

3. Under what conditions or circumstance may a divorced and remarried person hold the office of a deacon, elder, or pastor?

4. Practical Applications (chapter 10): Ask the class to take ten minutes to discuss these conclusions and select the three or four most important ones for practical use in church life.

Session 10, on Chapters 11-12:
The Gospel, Divorce, and the Church's Witness
in Marriage

1. What creates tension for the church when it seeks to minister to those going through divorce?

2. How did Jesus treat the law, and how could that be a pattern for the church today?

3. What arguments could be used against a position of enforced celibacy for divorced members?

4. In chapter 12: Considering that marriage is part of the created order and a necessity for humanity in general, how is a Christian marriage different from any other marriage? What is the church's greatest contribution to a couple's marriage?

5. The indicative mood in the Greek describes our position in Christ, for example, "We are risen with him." The imperative mood is one of command and potential. In what sense is the life and fruit of the Spirit (the indicative) essential for the fulfillment of the ethical commands regarding marriage?

Session 11, on Chapter 12:
The Church's Witness in Marriage, Preventing Divorce

1. How will the development of strength of character help to prevent divorce?

2. How can the church through its ministry develop strong convictions on marriage in its families?

3. How can the church lend support to those going through a divorce? Discuss how your class would envision a mini support group working in this.

4. What are suitable goals for a pastor in counseling an individual whose marriage is on the brink of separation?

5. What are the feelings of a church or pastor when, despite all they've done, the marriage breaks up? What can they still do to help?

Session 12, on Chapter 13:
The Church's Ministry in Divorce and Remarriage

1. In what way is it right to speak of the church having a theology for failure?

2. "Guilt has its place." What is its place?

3. Does divorce conclude the former union? How does this affect the future of the church's ministry to divorced members?

4. What is the foundation upon which remarriage may take place?

5. Do you agree with Dwight Small on the basis for the justification of remarriage?

6. How do you feel about the service of closure? How could it be adjusted to fit a local church situation?

7. How does personal confession of failure in one's marriage release the church more freely in its redemptive ministry toward those involved? How does this permit a stronger witness for the church to society at large?

8. What kinds of questions need to be dealt with by the couple who are planning on remarriage?

Session 13, on Chapter 14:
The Church's Educational Objectives in These Areas

1. Are there any areas where your attitudes toward those who have failed morally, or those attitudes of your church, fall short of those exemplified by Jesus?

2. Outline aspects of The Church's Role Under Grace. Discuss.

3. Let the class members share their experiences in shifting from harder attitudes to a greater sensitivity to the feelings and hurts of those divorced and their families.

4. As part of The Reeducation Process, assign some of the mentioned roles to two groups in your class. Have them get together the week before to plan a role-play for the session. If the class sits in a circle, members could be encouraged to jump into the role of one of the players. If they take it seriously, they will become involved in a sensitizing activity that can be both fun and educational. Take time to debrief feelings and learnings.

5. Select one or two class members to go to the local gospel bookstores to find sex education materials for use with children. The store manager might let them take materials out on consignment, to bring to class and comment on how they could be used in a family devotional time. Then they could be sold, or orders taken back to the store.

6. Concluding Statement: In paragraphs one and two there is reference to what the reader of the book ought to sense or realize. Go through these with your class and ask if they have made these steps in awareness and understanding. Have they found that "middle ground" mentioned in the final paragraph?

Notes

Chapter 1: *Jewish Marriage Customs and Patriarchy*

1. Gen. 29:15-30; Code of Hammurabi 137-141, dated 1728 to 1686 B.C.E., available in *ANET: Ancient Near Eastern Texts Relating to the Old Testament*, ed. by James B. Pritchard (Princeton, N.J., 1950), p. 172.

2. Abraham Cohen, *Everyman's Talmud* (New York: Schocken Books, 1975), p. 166.

3. Herbert Danby, *The Mishnah* (London: Oxford University Press, 1933), p. 233, Yebamoth 10.4-5; *The Dead Sea Scriptures*, trans. Theodor H. Gastner (Garden City, N.Y.: Doubleday, 1956), p. 66, The Zadokite Document 4.12—5.17.

4. George F. Moore, *Judaism in the First Centuries of the Christian Era*, 3 vols. (Cambridge: Harvard University Press, 1927, 1954), 2:119; cf. R. Ishmael's comment in *The Babylonian Talmud*, Seder Nashim, 4 vols. (1936), 4:29b.

5. One may assume the return of the dowry although this is not specifically mentioned in the Old Testament. Note the provision for return of dowry in the Code of Hammurabi 138 and in the Mishnah Ketuboth 8.8 and elsewhere; these chronologically bracket the Old Testament.

6. Cohen, pp. 162-163.

7. *Jewish Encyclopedia*, "Miun," 8:623f.

8. Cohen, p. 164, Kiddushin 2b.

9. Issac submitted to parental arrangement: Gen. 24. Esau showed independence: Gen. 26:34-35. Jacob submitted: Gen. 28:1-2. But Laban controlled the marriage of his daughters: Gen. 29:21-28.

10. Gittin 9.3 (Danby, p. 319).

11. For example, see Mishnah Gittin 9.4, which says that even with an invalid bill of divorce, the offspring of the next marriage is legitimate (Danby, p. 319).

12. Cf. Mishnah Gittin 7.5-6, where it appears that the wife is trying to persuade her husband to divorce her (Danby, p. 316).

13. Mishnah Gittin 9.10 (Danby, p. 321).

14. Note, for example, the research by Isaac Block, professor of contemporary ministries at Mennonite Brethren Bible College, Winnipeg, Manitoba, as reported by John Longhurst for the MCC Canada News Service in *Mennonite Weekly Review*, May 9, 1991, pp. 1-2: "Block also calls on Mennonites to examine the biblical concept of submission, which he says 'has been corrupted into a theology of dominance. . . . Are the values of permanence in marriage and the experience of personal safety and well-being of equal value, or should they be ranked? If they should be ranked, should personal safety rank higher than marriage if the marriage is abusive?' "

15. Lorne Shepherd, *Love Making His Way* (Toronto: Little Ones Books, Harmony Printing, 1985), p. 12.

16. Shepherd, p. 12. NRSV: "They too are also heirs of the gracious gift of life."

17. On this subject, see, for example, Eugene F. Roop, *Genesis*, in Believers Church Bible Commentary (Scottdale, Pa.: Herald Press, 1987), pp. 31-32, 45-49; Leonard Swidler, *Biblical Affirmations of Woman* (Philadelphia: Westminster Press, 1979); Charlotte H. Clinebell, *Meet Me in the Middle: On Becoming Human Together* (New York: Harper & Row, 1973); Letha Scanzoni and Nancy Hardesty, *All We're Meant to Be* (Waco, Tex.: Word Books, and Nashville: Abingdon, 1975); and a continuing stream of books.

18. Willard M. Swartley, *Slavery, Sabbath, War, and Women: Case Issues in Biblical Interpretation* (Scottdale, Pa.: Herald Press, 1983), p. 166; also see pp. 152-191, 256-275; Paul K. Jewett, *Man as Male and Female* (Grand Rapids, Mich.: Eerdmans, 1975).

Chapter 2: *Jewish Law on Divorce*

1. Boaz Cohen, *Roman and Jewish Law* (N.Y.: The Jewish Theological Seminary of America, 1966), p. 390. Cf. Koschaker, "Zur Interpretation des Art. 59 des Codex Bilalana," *Journal of Cuneiform Studies* 5 (1951): 104-122; The Laws of Eshnunna 25-30, in *ANET*, p. 162; Code of Hammurabi 138 in *ANET*, p. 172.

2. David Amram, *The Jewish Law of Divorce* (New York: Herman Press, 1975), p.22.

3. Cohen, p. 167.

4. Amram, p. 12.

5. Amram, p. 24.

6. J. H. Hertz, *The Pentateuch and the Haftorahs* (London: Soncino Press, 5727/1966), p. 850.

7. Amram, p. 33; Mishnah Gittin 9.10 (Herbert Danby, *The Mishnah* [London: Oxford University Press, 1933], p. 321); *Talmud Yerushalmi* (Krotoshin, 1886), Sotah 1.i (16b).

8. Mishnah Gittin 9.10 (Danby, p. 321).

9. Solomon Zeitlin, *Rise and Fall of the Judean State* (Philadelphia: The Jewish Publishing Society of America, 1967), p. 295.

10. *Philo Judaeus*, Special Laws Relating to Adultery 5, tr. by Yonge, in *Bohn's Antiquarian Library* (New York: AMS Press, reprint of 1892 ed.), 3:310-311.

11. Alfred Edersheim, *Sketches of Jewish Social Life* (Grand Rapids: Eerdmans, 1957), pp. 157-158.

12. Amram, p. 72; cf. Mishnah Gittin 7.7-9 (Danby, pp. 316-317).

13. Ketuboth 3.5 (Danby, p. 248).

14. Josephus, Antiquities of the Jews 4.8; Mishnah Ketuboth 3.4-5 (Danby, p. 248).

15. Amram, p. 44.
16. Mishnah Yebamoth 14.1 (Danby, p. 240); cf. Amram, p. 45.
17. Amram, p. 46: Maimonides in the treatise Gerushin 10.23.
18. Mishnah Ketuboth 4.8-9 (Danby, p. 250f.)
19. Mishnah Ketuboth 4.2, 4 (Danby, 249-250); Kiddushin 3.8 (Danby, p. 326).
20. Mishnah Yebamoth 13.1-2 (Danby, p. 237, with notes).
21. Amram, p. 84; Babylonian Talmud Makkoth 7a; Seder Nezikin 4.36f.
22. Amram, p. 43; cf. Mishnah Ketuboth 3.4-5; Sotah 5.1; 6:1-4 (Danby, pp. 248, 298-300).
23. Mishnah Sotah 5.1 (Danby, p. 298); "*Pornē,*" *Theological Dictionary of the New Testament,* ed. by G. Friedrich, vol. 6 (Grand Rapids, Mich.: Wm. B. Eerdmans, 1968), p. 592; cf. Test. Reuben 3:15 (R. H. Charles, *The Apocrypha and Pseudepigrapha of the Old Testament* [Oxford: Clarendon Press, 1913], 2:298).
24. Mishnah Ketuboth 3.5 (Danby, p. 248); Cohen, p. 167.
25. Amram, pp. 97-98; B. Talmud Ketuboth 77b.
26. B. Talmud Yebamoth 64a.
27. *Philo,* Special Laws Relating to Adultery 6 (tr. by Yonge, in *Bohn's A. L.,* 3:112).
28. Mishnah Nedarim 11.12; Ketuboth 5:5; Arakhin 5.6 (Danby, pp. 280, 252, 548); cf. Amram, pp. 56-59.
29. B. Talmud Ketuboth 110b.
30. Mishnah Gittin 9.8 (Danby, p. 320).
31. Amram, p. 76.
32. B. Talmud Gittin 90a-b.
33. Amram, pp. 38-39.
34. Amram, pp. 38-39.
35. Amram, pp. 79-80.
36. Amram, p. 113; this change was an ordinance by Shimean ben Shetah, as recorded in B. Shabbath 14b.
37. Responsa Asheri 42.1; Rabbi Moses Isserles 119.6; Amram, p. 52.
38. Amram, p. 101.
39. Mishnah Yebamoth 4.10 (Danby, p. 224).

Chapter 3: *The Pharisees and Jesus*
1. Asher Finkel, *The Pharisees and the Teacher of Nazareth* (Leiden: E. J. Brill, 1964), p. 47; cf. 1 Macc. 2:42-48.
2. Finkel, p. 143; Jerusalem Talmud, Shabboth 3b.
3. Finkel, pp. 135-136.
4. Mishnah Nedarim 4.3; Sotah 3.4 (Herbert Danby, *The Mishnah* [London: Oxford University Press, 1933], pp. 269, 296); cf. Luke 10:39.
5. Louis Finkelstein, *The Pharisees: The Sociological Background of Their Faith,* 2 vols. (Philadelphia: The Jewish Publication Society of America, 1938, 1962), 1:xlix.
6. Finkelstein, p. 99.
7. Finkelstein, 1:98.
8. Finkelstein, 1:98; cf. Assumption of Moses 7:4ff. (R. H. Charles, *The Apocrypha and Pseudepigrapha of the Old Testament* [Oxford: Clarendon Press, 1913], 2:419).
9. Finkelstein, 1:98-99.
10. George Foot Moore, *Judaism in the First Centuries of the Christian Era* (Cam-

bridge, Mass.: Harvard University Press, 1927), 2:192.

11. Finkelstein, 1:32 f.; cf. J. Talmud, Pesahim 49b.

12. Finkelstein, p. 38.

13. Finkel, *The Pharisees and the Teacher of Nazareth,* p. 143; J. Talmud Shabboth 3b.

Chapter 4: *Jesus, the Model of Caring for Sinners*

1. Cf. Matt.22:18; 23:13; Mark 12:13-15; 12:38-40; Luke 6:42; 11:43; 12:1; 13:15.

2. Cf. Matt. 9:10-11; 11:19; Luke 7:34; 18:9-14; 19:7.

3. Lev. 20:10; Deut. 22:21; Ezek. 16:38-40. This passage in John 8 does not have the support of the best manuscripts, but it is judged by many scholars to contain an ancient and valid tradition from the life of Jesus, probably from a non-Johannine origin. It is accepted as canonical by Catholics and most Protestants.

4. Donald Guthrie, *New Testament Introduction,* 3 vols. (Downer's Grove, Ill.: InterVarsity Press, 1978).

5. Werner Georg Kümmel, *Introduction to the New Testament* (London: SCM Press; Abingdon Press, 1975), pp. 44-52. Cf. also R. Bultmann and Karl Kundsin, *Form Criticism* (New York: Harper and Row, 1962).

6. Vincent Taylor, *The Gospel According to St. Mark* (London: Macmillan & Co., 1953), p. 415; Harry M. Orlinsky, *The Gospel According to St. Matthew,* vol. 2 of *The Synoptic Gospels* (New York: Ktav Publishing House, 1968), p. 258; regarding Klostermann, see Orlinski, ibid., pp. 261-262; W. C. Allen, *The Gospel According to St. Matthew,* 3d ed., in *The International Critical Commentary,* ed. by S. R. Driver, A. Plummer, and C. A. Briggs (Edinburgh: T. & T. Clark, 1912), pp. 202-203; and W. F. Albright and C. S. Mann, *Matthew,* vol. 28 of *The Anchor Bible,* ed. by W. F. Albright and D. N. Freedman (Garden City, N.Y.: Doubleday and Co., 1971), p. 225.

7. Redactional critics tend to suggest that "the Gospels offer us directly information about the theology of the early church and not about the actual teaching of the historical Jesus." Jack D. Kingsbury, for example, suggests that Matthew, in debate with the "Pharisee" on divorce, redacts or edits Mark's section on divorce (Mark 10:2-12) in order to emphasize that the will of God supersedes Moses in a manner stronger than Mark's presentation (*Matthew,* 2d ed., in *Proclamation Commentaries,* Minneapolis: Augsburg Fortress, 1986). Gunther Bornkamm held that Matthew was Mark's oldest exegete, while Krister Stendahl saw Matthew's Gospel as an advanced form of Jewish exegesis. Stendahl felt that Matthew had an appreciation of the Jewish context in which Jesus lived, that it was "a rich and wise book," but that his Gospel had a school of scribes behind it made up of teachers and church leaders (*The School of Matthew,* Lund: C. W. K. Gleerup, 1954).

8. Orlinski, *Matthew,* pp. 261-262.

9. R. Hugh Anderson, *The Gospel According to Mark,* in *New Century Bible,* ed. by E. Clements and Matthew Black (London: Oliphants, 1976), p. 240; D. E. Nineham, *The Gospel of St. Mark* (Baltimore, Md.:Penguin Books, 1963), pp. 259-260.

10. J. M. Rist, *On the Independence of Matthew* (Cambridge: Cambridge University Press, 1978), pp. 2, 102.

11. Ibid., pp. 106-107.

12. W. R. Farmer, *The Synoptic Problem* (N.Y.: Macmillan Publishing Co., 1964; Macon, Ga.: Mercer University Press, 1981).

13. B. C. Butler, *The Originality of St. Matthew* (Cambridge: Cambridge University Press, 1951), pp. 166-168; Louis Vaganay, *Le Probleme Synoptique*, Paris: Tournais, 1954.

14. Abel Isaksson, *Marriage and Ministry in the New Temple*, tr. by Neil Tomkinson (Copenhagen: C. W. K. Gleerup Land, 1965), p. 93.

15. Rudolf Bultmann, *Die Geschichte der Synoptischen Tradition* (Gottingen, 1958), quoted by J. Schmid in Isaksson, Ibid., p. 100.

16. Bultmann, *Geschichte*, 26, n. 1.

17. B. F. Streeter, *The Four Gospels: A Study of Origins* (London: Macmillan and Co., 1925), p. 259.

18. This discussion of the priorty of Matthew's divorce passage is based on a longer treatment in the author's unpublished thesis, "Scriptural Directions for Attitudes and Practices of Ministry Regarding Marriage, Divorce and Remarriage," Lutheran Theological Seminary, Saskatoon, Sask., May 1981.

Chapter 5: *Matthew 5 as Context for Matthew 19*
1. This will be discussed under Mt. 19:3ff.

2. Solomon Zeitlin, *The Rise and Fall of the Judean State* (Philadelphia: The Jewish Publishing Society of America, 1967), pp. 113-114.

Chapter 6: *Matthew 5:27-32*
1. In the Sermon on the Mount, Jesus speaks a word for the disciples, but so that all can hear. The *crowds* are mentioned in Matthew 5:1 and 7:28, bracketing the Sermon. Thus the Pharisees have access to Jesus' teachings on divorce in Matthew 5 and are ready to respond with the testing of Matthew 19.

2. Matthew does not include reference to a woman initiating divorce, as appears in Mark 10:12 and 1 Cor. 7:13. The latter reflect provisions of Roman law.

3. Frank Stagg in *General Articles, Matthew, Mark*, vol. 8 of *The Broadman Bible Commentary*, ed. by Clifton J. Allen (Nashville: Broadman Press, 1969), p. 110.

4. C. G. Montefiore, *The Synoptic Gospels*, 2nd ed. (London: Macmillan & Co., 1927), 2:66.

5. In *Broadman*, 8:110.

6. Bruce Vawter, "Divorce and the New Testament," *Catholic Biblical Quarterly* 39 (1977):530. On the point of mandatory divorce, see the following: David Amram, *The Jewish Law of Divorce* (New York: Herman Press, 1975), p. 43; and Mishnah Ketuboth 3.4-5, in Herbert Danby, *The Mishnah* (London: Oxford University Press, 1933), p. 248; also Hauck and Schulz, "*Pornē ktl.*," *Theological Dictionary of the New Testament* (TDNT), vol. 6, ed. by G. Kittel and G. Friedrich, tr. by G. W. Bromiley (Grand Rapids, Mich.: Eerdmans, 1968), p. 592.

7. A redaction is a change in the text to suit the thinking or theology of the church at a time subsequent to the original authorship.

8. "*Pornē*," TDNT, 6:592.

9. See Marlin Jeschke, *Discipling in the Church: Recovering a Ministry of the Gospel* (Scottdale, Pa.: Herald Press, 1973, 1988).

10. William Hendriksen, *Exposition to the Gospel According to Matthew, New Testament Commentary* (Grand Rapids: Baker Book House, 1973), p. 306.

Chapter 7: *Matthew 19:3-9*
1. W. C. Allen holds with this: *The Gospel According to St. Matthew*, 3d ed., in *The International Critical Commentary*, ed. by S. R. Driver, A. Plummer, and C. A. Briggs (Edinburg: T. & T. Clark, 1912), p. 202.

2. H. B. Swete supports this: *The Gospel According to St. Mark* (Grand Rapids: Eerdmans, 1952), p. 215.

3. In Mark 10:3 Jesus is portrayed as asking, "What did Moses command you?" In Matt. 19:7, it is the Pharisees who raise the question, "Why then did Moses command . . . ?" We have preferred Matthew's account over Mark's for its historical setting.

4. R. V. G. Tasker, *The Gospel According to St. Matthew,* in *The Tyndale New Testament Commentaries,* ed. by R. V. G. Tasker (Grand Rapids: Eerdmans, 1961), p. 181.

5. John Macquarrie, "The Nature of the Marriage Bond," *Theology* 78 (May 1975):230-236.

6. Cf. A. H. McNeile, *The Gospel According to St. Matthew* (London: Macmillan & Co., 1961), p. 274. "It cannot be supposed that Matthew wished to represent Jesus as siding with the school of Shammai." The close connection between vv. 8 and 9 shows Jesus is "emphasizing the ideal of creation, and any reference to Rabbinic disputes is beside the mark."

7. There is not good textual support for the latter part of v. 9 as it reads in the KJV: ". . . and whoso marrieth her which is put away doth commit adultery." However, Matt. 5:32 and Luke 16:18 carry this with adequate textual support. Probably copyists accommodated Matt. 19:9 to the prevailing text of 5:32.

8. Refer to Exod. 21:7-11 and Deut. 21:10-14 to see further scriptural basis for remarriage of the victimized wife.

9. See Deut. 24:1-4; Mishnah Gittin, whole tractate, especially 4.1-2 on annuling or rendering void or invalid a bill of divorce; 8.4 (Herbert Danby, *The Mishnah* [London: Oxford University Press, 1933], pp. 307-321).

10. One of the better articles on the different views of the excepting clause has been that of H. G. Coiner, "Those 'Divorce and Remarriage' Passages," *Concordia Theological Monthly* 39 (June 1968): 367-384.

11. J. A. Fitzmyer, " The Matthean Divorce Texts and Some New Palestinian Evidence," *Theological Studies* 37 (1976): 210 is representative.

12. Coiner, "Those . . . Passages," pp. 373-374.

13. Abel Isaksson, *Marriage and Ministry in the New Temple,* tr. by Neil Tomkinson (Copenhagen: C. W. K. Gleerup Land, 1965), pp. 139-142.

14. Guy Duty has arrived at this interpretation in his book, which has greatly influenced the Assemblies of God, U.S.A. Guy Duty, *Divorce and Remarriage* (Minneapolis: Bethany, 1967), p. 35.

15. Amram, *Jewish Law,* p. 43; Mishnah Ketuboth 3.4-5 (Danby, p. 248); Friedrich Hauck and Sigfried Schulz, *"Pornē ktl.," Theological Dictionary of the New Testament* (TDNT), vol. 6, ed. by G. Kittel and G. Friedrich, tr. by G. W. Bromiley (Grand Rapids, Mich.: Eerdmans, 1968), p. 592.

16. F. W. Beare, *The Earliest Records of Jesus* (Oxford: Basil Blackwell, 1962), pp. 192-193.

17. Coiner, "Those . . . Passages," p. 377, citing Hauck and Schulz, *"Pornē ktl.," TDNT,* 6:591-592.

18. See in chapter 2, Jewish Law and Divorce, at subhead Divorce Replaces Stoning, and supporting note.

Chapter 8: *Matthew 19:10-12*

1. See the following for further discussion of the Roman Catholic viewpoints: Jerome Kodell, "The Celibacy Logian in Matthew 9:12," *Biblical Theological Bulletin* 8 (no. 1):19-23; Q. Quesnel, "Made Themselves Eunuchs for the King-

dom of Heaven," *Catholic Biblical Quarterly* 30 (1968): 335-336.

2. Kodell, "The Celibacy Logian," pp. 19-23.

3. Coiner, "Those Divorce and Remarriage Passages," *Concordia Theological Monthly* 39 (June 1968), p. 379.

Chapter 9: *Studies from the Letters*

1. See 1 Cor. 7:1, 25; 8:1; 12:1; 16:1, 12; cf. quotes from them in 6:12 and the reports of 1:11-12; 5:1.

2. See 1 Tim. 4:1-5; cf. the apocryphal Acts of Thomas 1:12-14; Rev. 14:4 is likely meant metaphorically, but some readers might have taken it in a literal sense.

3. See Walter Schmithals, *Gnosticism in Corinth* (Nashville: Abingdon Press, 1971) for a study of this possibility. Gnostic systems are well documented in the second century A.D. and later.

4. See Gordon D. Fee, *The First Epistle to the Corinthians,* in *The New International Commentary on the New Testament,* ed. by F. F. Bruce (Grand Rapids, Mich.: Eerdmans, 1987), pp. 10-15.

5. Ibid., p. 12.

6. M. C. Tenney, *The Zondervan Pictorial Encyclopedia of the Bible,* vol. 1 (Grand Rapids: Zondervan, 1975), p. 1975; Fee, pp. 2-3.

7. A. Robertson and A. Plummer, *Commentary on the First Epistle of St. Paul to the Corinthians, 2d ed.,* in *The International Critical Commentary,* ed. by C. A. Briggs et al. (Edinburgh: T. & T. Clark, 1916), p. 139.

8. J. A. Crook, *Law and Life of Rome* (London: Thames & Hudson, 1970), p. 105.

9. C. K. Barrett, *A Commentary on the First Epistle to the Corinthians* (London: A. & C. Black, 1971), p. 165.

10. Hans Conzelmann, *1 Corinthians,* in *Hermeneia—A Critical and Historical Commentary on the Bible* (Philadelphia: Fortress Press, 1975), p. 122.

11. The following are a few of the scholars who concur on this: R. C. H. Lenski, C. K. Barrett, Jean Hering, Leon Morris, H. L. Goudge, A. W. Meyer, Wm. F. Orr, and James A. Walther.

12. Martin Luther, *First Corinthians,* in *Luther's Works* (St. Louis: Concordia, 1973), p. 36.

13. A. Robertson and A. Plummer, Chas. Eerdman, and Walter Koehler hold this position.

14. Sakae Kubo, "1 Corinthians 7:16: Optimistic or Pessimistic?" *New Testament Studies* 24 (July 1978), pp. 543-544. This in v. 16 is similar in translation to the New American Standard Revised Version.

15. Conzelmann, *1 Corinthians,* pp. 123-124.

16. This position is supported by Fee, pp. 331-332, as fitting the context.

17. John Murray, *Divorce* (Philadelphia: The Committee on Christian Education, The Orthodox Presbyterian Church, 1953), p. 79.

18. On this, see the discussion in *The Interpreter's Bible,* ed. by George A. Buttrick (Nashville: Abingdon, 1955), 11:410-413: Does this mean not to have a leader who is remarried after divorce from an unbeliever, or one who is remarried after the death of the spouse, or both? The view of the patristic period (after the first century) was that it meant the leader must not remarry after the death of the spouse (cf. Rom 7:2.). There is no thought here of concubinage, polygamy, and remarriage after divorce from a Christian spouse, practices prohibited to all believers. In the ascetic environment around the author of the pastoral epistles,

"married only once" may have seemed rather generous. In the ancient church, there was a trend toward celibacy of the clergy.

19. Representative of this view are E. Glenn Hinson in *The Broadman Bible Commentary*, vol. 11, ed. by Clifton J. Allen (Nashville, Tenn.: Broadman Press, 1971), p. 317; and John Calvin, *Commentaries on the Epistle to Timothy, Titus and Philemon*, tr. by Wm. Pringle (Grand Rapids, Mich.: Eerdmans, 1942), pp. 77-78.

20. Pat E. Harrell, *Divorce and Remarriage in the Early Church* (Austin, Tex.: R. B. Swete, 1967), p. 53.

21. Homer A. Kent, Jr., *The Pastoral Epistles* (Chicago: Moody Press, 1958), p. 129.

22. Stanley A. Ellisen, *Divorce and Remarriage in the Church* (Grand Rapids: Zondervan Publishing House, 1977), pp. 81-83, 87-88.

Chapter 11: *The Gospel and Divorce*
1. Harold Haas, *Marriage* (Philadelphia: Muhlenberg Press, 1960), p. 40. Cf. Matt. 19:21; 5:39-41; Luke 9:60.

2. Dwight H. Small, *The Right to Remarry* (Old Tappan, N. J.: Revell, 1975), p. 187.

3. See Mishnah Ketubah 5.1; 8.8; 9.9; Mishnah Gittin 4.3; 5.1-3; available in *The Mishnah*, tr. by Herbert Danby (London: Oxford University Press, 1933).

4. This legal context appears in Mark 10:12 and 1 Cor. 7:10, 13.

Chapter 12: *The Church's Witness in Marriage*
1. Walter J. Koehler, "The Constitutive Nature of Marriage" (S. T. M. Thesis, Concordia Seminary, St. Louis, Mo., May 1966), p. 9.

2. Ibid., p. 12.

3. Harold Haas, *Marriage* (Philadelphia: Muhlenberg Press, 1960), p. 26.

4. C. W. Scudder, *The Family in Christian Perspective* (Nashville, Tenn.: Broadman Press, 1972), p. 24.

5. C. S. Lewis, *Mere Christianity* (New York: Macmillan Co., 1958), p. 81.

6. Scudder, p. 27.

7. Richard Bondi, "Notes on the Theology of Marriage," *Pastoral Psychology* 25 (Summer 1977): 294-304, especially p. 300.

8. Helmut Thielicke, *Theological Ethics* (Philadelphia: Fortress Press, 1966), p. 43.

9. Ibid., p. 43; cf. 1 Cor. 10:11.

10. Ibid., p. 52.

11. Scudder, *Family in Christian Perspective*, p. 7.

12. Thielicke, *Theological Ethics*, p. 69.

13. 1 Cor. 10:11. For a comparison of the indicative and imperative in Paul, see Rom. 6:1-7; 8:1-17; Gal. 3:13-25; and 1 Cor. 6:9-11. Cf. Thielicke, *Theological Ethics*, pp. 70-71.

14. J. Peterson and E. Smith, *Before You Marry* (Wheaton: Tyndale House, 1974); Norman Wright, *Premarital Counseling* (Chicago: Moody Press, 1977). Other good premarital counseling programs are available, too.

15. Peterson and Smith, p. 12.

16. Ed Wheat, *Love Life for Every Married Couple* (Grand Rapids, Mich.: Zondervan: 1980, pp. 177-202.

17. See, for example, *The Mennonite Hymnal* (Scottdale, Pa.: Herald Press, 1969), no. 728: "With joy we identify with you in this high moment of commitment and covenant. The vows you have taken compel us to weigh the purity of

our love and to strengthen the relationships of our homes. We pledge that, as you follow Christ, we will join you in seeking to apprehend Him as our true life, and in serving Him by our love. We offer our prayers that your lives may become increasingly rich in understanding, in common loyalties, and in useful vocation. We thank God for the home you now establish, and anticipate its strength, influence, and support of the church in its mission."

18. Jay E. Adams, *The Christian Counselor's Manual* (Nutley, N.J.: Presbyterian and Reformed Publ. Co., 1973), pp. 228-229.

19. Ibid., p. 230.

20. Bernard Harnik, *Risk and Chance in Marriage* (Waco, Tex.: Word Books, 1972), pp. 1-30.

21. Ibid., pp. 66f.

22. For an excellent annotated resource guide, see Gordon K. Franklin's *Marriage, Divorce and Remarriage: A Resource Guide* (13427-40th. St., Edmonton, Alta.: C. I. Seminars, 1980).

23. Family Life Publications, Inc. Box 427, Saluda, NC 28773.

24. Gene Getz, *The Measure of a Marriage*, and *The Measure of a Marriage Workbook* (Ventura, Calif.: Regal Books, Gospel Light Publications, 1980).

25. Ed Wheat, *Love Life for Every Married Couple* (Grand Rapids: Zondervan, 1980).

26. Ibid., p. 249; A. K. Carroll, *From the Brink of Divorce* (Garden City, N.Y.: Doubleday-Galilee Original, 1978).

27. Ed Wheat, *Intended for Pleasure* (New York: Fleming Revell, 1977).

28. David and V. Mace, *How to Have a Happy Marriage* (Nashville: Abingdon Press, 1983); Norman Wright, *The Pillars of Marriage* (Glendale: Regal Books, Gospel Light Publishers, 1979).

29. Ed Wheat, *Love Life*, chap. 15, "How to Save Your Marriage Alone," pp. 203-236.

30. For a helpful discussion on causes see G. Dahl, *Why Christian Marriages Break Up* (Nashville: Nelson Publishers, 1979).

31. Louise Despert, *Children of Divorce* (New York: Doubleday, 1953); Rabbi Earl Grollman, *Explaining Divorce to Children* (Boston: Beacon Press, 1972); H. S. Vigeveno and A. Claire, *Divorce and the Children* (Glendale: Regal Books, 1979).

Chapter 13: *The Church's Ministry in Divorce and Remarriage*

1. Frank C. Peters, "Redemptive Realism in Dealing with Divorce and Remarriage," p. 8.

2. Ibid.

3. Helmut Thielicke, *The Ethics of Sex*, tr. by J. W. Doberstein (Greenwood, S.C.: Attic Press, 1964), p. 171f.

4. Dwight Small, *The Right to Remarry* (Old Tappan, N.J.: Revell, 1975), p. 178.

5. See chapters 5-6, above.

6. Dwight Small, *The Right to Remarry*, p. 179.

7. John Milton, *The Complete Poetry and Selected Prose of John Milton* (New York: Random House, 1950), p. 652.

8. James Castelli, *What the Church Is Doing for Divorced and Remarried Catholics* (Chicago: Claretian Publications, 1978), p. 27.

9. Small, *The Right to Remarry*, p. 183.

10. William J. Gaither, "Gentle Shepherd," *Hymns for the Family of God* (Nashville, Tenn.: Paragon Associates, 1976), 596.

11. Edwin Bontrager, *Divorce and the Faithful Church* (Scottdale, Pa.: Herald Press, 1978), p. 143.

12. Reformed Church of America, proceedings of the General Synod, "Biblical Perspectives on Marriage, Divorce, and Remarriage" (1975), p. 170.

13. Harold Haas, *Marriage* (Philadelphia: Muhlenberg Press, 1960), p. 42; Minutes, The United Lutheran Church of America, 1956.

14. Illinois Mennonite Conference, Freeport, Ill., Spring 1990, "Statement on Divorce and Remarriage," *Missionary Guide* 47 (June 1990, no. 1): 2.

15. Several alternative policies are considered by Bontrager in *Divorce and the Faithful Church*, pp. 156-160.

16. Small, *Right to Remarry*, p. 186.

17. Taken from *Ritual in a New Day* (Nashville: Abingdon, 1976), p. 84, based on a prayer of confession in a wedding celebration in Sharon N. Emswiler and Thomas N. Emswiler, *Women and Worship* (New York: Harper & Row, 1974), pp. 95-97. *Ritual in a New Day* contains several rituals of closure for divorce which could be adapted to local situations.

18. There are many good counseling books on reconciliation. That vital process is not the purpose of this book, but rather to assist the church in the event that all efforts at reconciliation have failed.

19. For help for children of divorce, see H. S. Vigeveno and Anne Claire, *Divorce and the Children* (Glendale: Regal Books, 1979); Earl A. Grollman, *Explaining Divorce to Children* (Kansas City: Beacon Hill Press, 1969).

20. John R. Martin, *Divorce and Remarriage* (Scottdale, Pa.: Herald Press, 1974); L. Woodson, *Divorce and the Gospel of Grace* (Waco, Tex.: Word Books, 1978).

21. David K. Switzer, *The Minister as Crisis Counselor* (Nashville: Abingdon Press, 1974); Norman Wright, *An Answer to Divorce* (Los Angeles: Harvest House, 1977); Bob W. Brown, *Getting Married Again: A Christian Guide for Successful Remarriage* (Waco, Tex.: Word Publishers, 1978); Jim Smoke, *Growing Through Divorce* (Los Angeles: Harvest House, 1976); Arnold W. D. Baird and E. Vaughn, *Divorce, Prevention or Survival* (Philadelphia: Westminster Press, 1977); Gary Collins, *It's Okay to Be Single* (New York: Continental Congress, 1976).

22. For an example of these, see: Richard Krebs, *Alone Again* (Minneapolis: Augsburg Press, 1968); Darlene McRoberts, *Second Marriage* (Minneapolis: Augsburg Press, 1978); Suzanne Stewart, *Parent Alone* (Waco, Tex.: Word Books, 1979); Suzanne Stewart, *Divorced! I Wouldn't Have Given a Nickel for Your Chances* (Grand Rapids: Zondervan, 1976).

23. For a discussion of these various denominational positions, see Bontrager, *Divorce and the Faithful Church*, pp. 66-113; or James G. Emerson, *Divorce, the Church and Remarriage* (Philadelphia: Westminster Press, 1952), pp. 109-147.

Chapter 14: *The Church's Educational Objectives in These Areas*

1. The author has prepared an unpublished eight-module series designed to produce sensitivity and understanding for those who have experienced divorce: "Church Seminars: Marriage and Divorce in the Church," by George R. Ewald, c/o Living Faith Community Church, 530 Victoria Ave., Chatham, Ont. N7L 3B6, Canada.

2. Joseph Epstein, *Divorce in America* (New York: E. P. Dutton, 1975), p. 19.

3. Ibid., p. 92.

4. Lars Granberg, "Divorce and Remarriage: Practical Implications for the Church," in *Make More of Your Marriage*, ed. Gary R. Collins (Waco, Tex.: Word Books, 1976), p. 100.

5. Ibid., p. 102.

6. On celibacy, Jesus said, "Let anyone accept this who can" (Matt. 19:12);

and Paul said, "Each has a particular gift from God" (1 Cor. 7:7). These sayings do not enforce celibacy.

7. Excellent assistance on role-playing and values can be found in the following: Robert C. Hawley, *Value Exploration Through Role-Playing* (New York: Hart Publishing, 1975), pp. 24-45, 117-125; Sidney Simon, Leland Howe, and Howard Kirschenbaum, *Values-Clarification* (New York: Hart Publishing, 1972).

8. B. Reed, *Single on Sunday: A Manual for Successful Single Adult Ministries* (Grand Rapids: Baker Book House, 1978); L. Woodson, *Divorce and the Gospel of Grace* (Waco, Tex.: Word Books, 1978).

Bibliography

Historical Background

Amram, David. *The Jewish Law of Divorce*. New York: Herman Press, 1975.

Bowker, John. *Jesus and the Pharisees*. Cambridge: University Press, 1973.

Edersheim, Alfred. *Sketches of Jewish Social Life*. Grand Rapids: Eerdmans, 1957.

Finkel, Asher. *The Pharisees and the Teacher of Nazareth*. Leiden: E. J. Brill, 1964.

Finkelstein, Louis. *The Pharisees: The Sociological Background of Their Faith*. 2 vols. Philadelphia: The Jewish Publication Society of America, 1938, 1962.

Harrell, Pat E. *Divorce and Remarriage in the Early Church*. Austin, Tex.: R. B. Swete, 1967.

Mace, David. *Hebrew Marriage*. London: Epworth Press, 1953.

General Resources on Divorce

Bontrager, G. Edwin. *Divorce and the Faithful Church*. Scottdale, Pa.: Herald Press, 1978.

Coiner, H. G. "Those 'Divorce and Remarriage' Passages." *Concordia Theological Monthly* 39 (June 1968): 367-384.

Emerson, James G. *Divorce, the Church and Remarriage*. Philadelphia: Westminster Press, 1961.

Haas, Harold. *Marriage*. Philadelphia: Muhlenberg Press, 1960.

Koehler, Walter J. "The Constitutive Nature of a Christian Marriage." S.T.M. Thesis, Concordia Seminary, St. Louis, Mo. May 1966.

Martin, John R. *Divorce and Remarriage*. Scottdale, Pa.: Herald Press, 1974.

Murray, John. *Divorce*. Philadelphia: Presbyterian and Reformed Publishers, 1976.

Shaner, Donald W. *A Christan View of Divorce*. Leiden: E. J. Brill, 1969.

Small, Dwight H. *The Right to Remarry*. Old Tappan, N.J.: Revell, 1975.

Resources on Ethics

Bonhoeffer, Dietrich. *Ethics,* ed. by E. Bethge. N.Y.: Macmillan Publishers, 1955; German Edition, 1949.

Brunner, Emil. *The Divine Imperative*. Philadelphia: Westminster Press, 1947.

Hordern, William. *Living by Grace*. Philadelphia: Westminster Press, 1975.

Thielicke, Helmut. *The Ethics of Sex*. N.Y.: Harper and Row, 1964.

———————————. *Theological Ethics*. Philadelphia: Fortress Press, 1966.

Resources for Practical Applications

Augsburger, A. Don. *Marriages That Work*. Scottdale, Pa.: Herald Press, 1984.

Baird, Arnold W. D., and E. Vaughn. *Divorce, Prevention or Survival*. Philadelphia: Westminster Press, 1977.

Bohannan, Paul. *Divorce and After*. Garden City, N.J.: Doubleday and Co., 1970.

Brown, Bob W. *Getting Married Again: A Christian Guide for Successful Remarriage*. Waco, Tex.: Word Books Publ., 1978.

Castelli, James. *What the Church Is Doing for Divorced and Remarried Catholics*. Chicago: Claretian Publishers, 1978.

Collins, Gary R. *It's Okay to Be Single*. N.Y.: Continental Congress, 1976.

_____, ed. *Make More of Your Marriage*. Waco, Tex.: Word Books, 1976.

Dahl, G. *Why Christian Marriages Are Breaking Up*. Knoxville: Nelson Publ., 1979.

De Santo, Charles P., and Terri Robinson Williams. *Putting Love to Work in Marriage*. Scottdale, Pa.: Herald Press, 1988.

Ellison, Stanley A. *Divorce and Remarriage in the Church*. Grand Rapids: Zondervan, 1977.

Epstein, Joseph. *Divorce in America*. N.Y.: E. P. Dutton, 1975.

Fairfield, James G. T. *When You Don't Agree*. Scottdale, Pa.: Herald Press, 1977.

Grollman, Earl A. *Explaining Divorce to Children*. Kansas City: Beacon Hill Press, 1969.

Harnik, Bernard. *Risk and Chance in Marriage*. Waco, Tex.: Word Books, 1972.

Hunt, Richard A. "The Minister and Divorce Crisis," in *The Minister as Crisis Counselor*, by David K. Switzer. Nashville: Abingdon Press, 1974.

Krebs, Richard. *Alone Again*. Minneapolis: Augsburg Press, 1978.

LaHaye, Timothy. *How to Be Happy Though Married*. Grand Rapids: Zondervan, 1973.

McRoberts, Darlene. *Second Marriage*. Minneapolis: Augsburg Press, 1978.

Peterson, J. and E. Smith. *Before You Marry*. Wheaton: Tyndale House, 1974.

Reed, B. *Single on Sunday: A Manual for Successful Single Adult Ministries*. Grand Rapids: Baker Book House, 1978.

Roberts, W., and Norman Wright. *Before You Say I Do*. Los Angeles: Harvest House, 1976.

Schmitt, Abraham and Dorothy. *Renewing Family Life*. Scottdale, Pa.: Herald Press, 1985.

_____. *Renewing Family Life Video/Book Unit*. Scottdale, Pa.: Herald Press, 1986.

Scudder, C. W. *The Family in Christian Perspective.* Nashville: Broadman Press, 1972.

Stewart, Suzanne. *Divorced! I Wouldn't Have Given a Nickle for Your Chances.* Grand Rapids: Zondervan, 1976.

Vigeveno, H. S. and Claire, Anne. *Divorce and Children.* Glendale, Calif.: Regal Books Division, Gospel Light Publications, 1979.

Wenger, J. C. *Dealing Redemptively with Those Involved in Divorce and Remarriage Problems.* Scottdale, Pa.: Herald Press, 1965.

Woodson, L. *Divorce and the Gospel of Grace.* Waco, Tex.: Word Books, 1978.

Wright, Norman. *The Pillars of Marriage.* Glendale: Regal Books, Gospel Light Publications, 1979.

_____. *Premarital Counseling.* Chicago: Moody Press, 1977.

Scripture Index

General Index

The Author

George R. Ewald was born in Hamilton, Ontario. He served in pastoral ministry in six different pastorates for a total of twenty-three years. Four of these were with the Pentecostal Assemblies of Canada, one with the Baptist Convention of Ontario and Quebec, and the most recent was a seven-year interdenominational ministry with the Living Faith Community Church, in Chatham, Ontario.

His pastoral experience included street ministry, seven years of drive-in services, television and radio outreach, work with district executives, camp evangelist and teacher, and participation on national denominational committees dealing with divorce, evangelism, ministry of women, Bible colleges, and men's fellowships.

For eleven years, Ewald was lecturer in Bible, evangelism,

85468

counseling, and practical theology at the Eastern Pentecostal Bible College, Peterborough, Ontario. He graduated from that same college and has a B.A. in Bible from Wheaton (Illinois) College and a Master of Sacred Theology (S.T.M.) from the Lutheran Theological Seminary in Saskatoon, Saskatechwan.

George and his wife, Shirley (Gordon), were married in 1954. They have three children (Colleen, George, and Andrea) and six grandchildren. They are members of Living Faith Community Church, Chatham, Ontario.

In 1989 Ewald resigned from his last pastorate to give himself to a ministry of renewal in the church at large. His speciality is leading church seminars dealing with marriage enrichment, divorce ministry, and spiritual fitness. He resides in Chatham, Ontario. Mail can reach him c/o Living Faith Community Church, 530 Victoria Avenue, Chatham, Ontario N7L 3B6, and his telephone number is 519 354-6115.